Charismata: God's Gifts
for God's People

Biblical Perspectives on Current Issues

Howard Clark Kee, General Editor

Charismata: God's Gifts for God's People

by John Koenig

The Westminster Press
Philadelphia

Scripture quotations from the Revised Standard Version of The Holy Bible, Old Testament, Copyright 1952; New Testament, First Edition, Copyright 1946; New Testament, Second Edition, © 1972, by the Division of Christian Education of the National Council of the Churches of Christ in the U.S.A. Used by permission.

First edition

PUBLISHED BY THE WESTMINSTER PRESS®

Philadelphia, Pennsylvania

Printed in the United States of America

9 8 7 6 5 4 3 2 1

To Elisabeth

Library of Congress Cataloging in Publication Data

Koenig, John T   1938–
    Charismata : God's gifts for God's people.

    (Biblical perspectives on current issues series)
    Includes bibliographical references and index.
    1. Gifts, Spiritual—Biblical teaching. 2. Spiritual life—Lutheran authors. 3. Pentecostalism.
I. Title. II. Series.
BS680.G5K63   234'.1   77—12700
ISBN 0–664–24176–X

CONTENTS

EDITOR'S PREFACE

Ours is an era characterized by a divided mind. I am not speaking of the perennial divisions between old and young, between conservative and liberal, or even between spiritual and material values. Rather, I would draw attention to a fundamental tension within individuals between a yearning to be involved and a longing to be left alone. A young couple of my acquaintance complained that they were going to have to withdraw from their fifth experiment in communal living: "It's the other people who are always the problem." Disenchanted with communes, the pair now are living in California, where they can contemplate the Pacific, in isolation and perhaps in peace.

The twin urges for group involvement and private experience are evident in contemporary religious life as well. The growth of evangelical groups and churches in this country has been astonishing, as has been the phenomenal sale of books that combine science fiction and apocalyptic hopes for a new age. The appeal of the evangelical revival is twofold: on the one hand, it fosters a sense of group identity with persons who regard themselves as having been granted special insights and powers by God which enable them to share in the outworking of God's plan. At the same time, they are able to accept rejection and scorn by their fellow human beings, since they are confident of their ultimate vindication by God. On the other hand, the evangelicals foster free expression of personal religious experience. The free manifestation of Christian commitment may well exhibit the variety of actions known in the church's tradition as *charismatic gifts.* In past centuries these public expressions of personal experience have been limited largely to members of what other Christians have disdainfully called sects or fringe groups.

Today, however, such experiences are increasingly evident among main-line Protestant denominations and Roman Catholics as well. This is in part the result of church people—Protestant and Catholic—having rediscovered the Bible, stimulated by modern speech translations, which continue to sell by the millions.

In reading the New Testament, especially Paul's letters, new or retooled Christians have discovered that the Spirit of God was a free-moving force in the early church. One of the sure signs of God's favor on newly founded Christianity was thought to be the extraordinary gifts that accompanied the work of the Spirit within the lives of converts to the new movement. As is well known, the gifts included speaking in tongues (apparently the utterance of ecstatic speech), the ability to perform healings, and making pronouncements by the authority of Christ for the guidance of the church. From New Testament times down to our own, however, such manifestations of the Spirit have been viewed with suspicion by those responsible for order and structure in the churches. Some critics regarded these "gifts" as unbridled emotional outbursts; others sought to suppress them as a threat to peace and order in the life of the churches. A gnawing anxiety remains: are such seemingly spontaneous phenomena really the work of God?

So long as these displays of the Spirit were restricted to the so-called Pentecostal wing of the church, most Christians felt that the question could be ignored. That is no longer possible. The pervasiveness of the charismatic gifts among the churches requires that every thoughtful Christian come to terms with them. Are they as essential to the life of the church today as they obviously were in apostolic times? If so, why are they still viewed with suspicion or hostility in many churches today? Are they dismissed today because the freedom of the Spirit might upset our hallowed habit patterns of worship and fellowship? Is God seeking to convey a new, relevant message to the churches through the charismatic manifestations?

John Koenig combines expertise as a New Testament scholar with a sympathetic investigation of the charismatic movement. He offers a careful study of the origins of the spiritual gifts and perceptive observations about the place of the charismatic movement in the life of the church today. In so doing, he suggests how our current yearning for group identity and for private experiential expression converge in this significant Christian phenomenon.

HOWARD CLARK KEE

Bryn Mawr, Pennsylvania

Charismata: A Gracious Challenge?

There is a great perplexity abroad in the church today about the gifts of God. In America it arises chiefly as a response by members of the traditional denominations (Presbyterian, Methodist, Lutheran, Episcopalian, United Church of Christ, Baptist, Roman Catholic, etc.) to the steady growth within their ranks of diverse movements called "charismatic." By now, most of us traditional Christians who are not affiliated with such groups know at least a few people who have joined them, perhaps in our own congregations.

Such Christians invariably feel that they have received unusual blessings from God through the Holy Spirit. These ordinarily include the ability to pray in unintelligible but profoundly meaningful tongues (glossolalia); physical and emotional healings; the hearing of personally relevant prophecies and/or the call to speak prophetically to others. Most of all, however, these believers claim to have undergone a dramatic renewal or heightening of their faith which produces a "closer walk with the Lord" than they have previously known.

Those of us who are acquainted with such renewed Christians find that they differ widely in temperament, just as other believers do. Some are effervescent, some thoughtful. While a few appear pushy or fiercely intent upon converting their friends and relatives, others seem extraordinarily loving and patient. After interviewing scores of Christians who speak in tongues, a minister-psychologist concludes that they exhibit no more neurotic tendencies than other church members.[1] Glossolalia therefore ought not to be summarily dismissed as a pathological practice. Likewise, from a sociological point of view, it would be simplistic to understand the various charismatic movements primarily as a ground swell of popular dissatisfaction with current ecclesiastical bureaucracies.[2] Nor do we have sufficient evidence to conclude that charismatic renewal represents the latest passing fad in American religion, like the "death of God" fiasco or the Jesus movement of the late '60s.[3]

Just when we find ourselves unable to wrap charismatic groups and individuals in neat, manageable packages, the real questions emerge. For then we traditional Christians must begin to ask: What does this mysterious giftedness mean to *us?* Do those people have something that we don't have, but ought to? If we allow such questions more than fleeting access to our consciousness, our emotional lives are likely to become quite complex. Insofar as we meet socially with "renewed" Christians, we shall probably feel a disconcerting blend of fear, admiration, hostility, envy, and love. We may find ourselves haunted by reflections such as the following:

> Why do some of these people appear to think of me as a second-class Christian? How dare they judge my spirituality! Or is it I who am judging my spirituality in the light of their obvious enthusiasm? And why am I so attracted to some of them? Can it be that their treasures are genuine, though described in language that I sometimes find excessive? On the other hand, they surely presume too much in claiming such an intimate relationship with God. Have they no respect for his transcendence? Besides, I know of Christians as spiritual as they are who do not call themselves charismatics. I would feel more comfortable modeling my life after these traditional saintly figures than after the superficiality I see in many of the "renewed" people.

> Add to this another problem. I just don't like arrangements in which I'm doing all the receiving. That's downright unchristian. Still, I must account for the gifts which charismatic groups experience, not to mention the Biblical evidence they cite for charismatic practices in the first-century church. Can it be that God is pouring out such gifts today, even on people whose

temperaments and intellects I may dislike? If so, how necessary are they for mature Christian life? Shall I seek these gifts, knowing full well that my quest may turn out to be a selfish one bent on the accumulation of personal power? Or shall I try to grow spiritually in some other way?

The study that follows proceeds from a conviction that we traditional Christians have much to gain from a closer look at the charismatic experience of the New Testament church. Only in this way, I believe, can we find the "space" to confront our own hearts and minds honestly on the issue of God's gifts. To put the matter in theological terms, God's word, contained in the Scriptures, gives us a place to stand. It will seldom shelter us from conflict, and it will never excuse us from the necessity of making decisions. But it will enlarge the whole process of discernment by tempering our momentary hopes and fears with its eternal wisdom. A Biblical study of God's gifts offers us the possibility of stepping back somewhat from the pressures of contemporary Christian experience so as to share reflectively in an ancient Christian experience. It gives us another opinion than the hot, but frequently distorted data furnished by our emotional reactions to current phenomena. Through studying the Biblical material, we may be enabled to make a distinction that is difficult to bring off on our own in everyday life: namely, to separate gifts from the less than perfect human beings in whom they appear long enough to ask ourselves what God intends to communicate to us today *via the gifts*.[4]

Here, however, I must add a proviso. As a student and professional teacher of the New Testament, I would be among the first to admit that not even approaching an ancient text with empathy and the best of historical methodologies guarantees that its truth will take hold in our lives. Over the centuries traditional Christian theology has wisely maintained that true, experiential understanding comes only from the Holy Spirit, who operates through our conversations with the Biblical writers. As Kierkegaard reminds us, we must call upon God himself to "heal the misunderstanding heart by the understanding of the word, to understand the word."[5] Still, we must first *encounter* that word, so Biblical study is probably our best point of departure, especially if our believing imaginations have already been grasped by those very gifts of God which we seek, with his help, to comprehend. To such readers, who find themselves painfully aware of their own need for growth and hopeful that God's gifts will nourish them, but who at the same time feel skeptical about the beliefs and practices of Christian communities that call themselves charismatic, this book is offered.

Before we plunge into the Biblical material, however, some definitions and explanations are in order. The first word in our title, "charismata," is the plural form of the well-known Greek noun *charisma*. The apostle Paul especially uses it to describe gifts of God (not always spectacular) that differentiate believing individuals from one another for the purpose of enhancing their mutual service. In Paul's view, every Christian has been granted at least one of these personalized gifts (I Cor. 7:7). The frequently encountered word "charismatic," which today refers to either a gift or a gifted person, does not occur in the Bible. We may, however, use the word in good faith, provided that we allow its meaning to derive from what the New Testament writers tell us about charismata.

The second part of our title, "God's gifts for God's people," I have borrowed from the eucharistic liturgy contained in *The Draft Proposed Book of Common Prayer* of the Episcopal Church. There we read that after consecrating the bread and wine, the celebrant sets them before prospective communicants by proclaiming: "The gifts of God for the people of God."[6] My intention is to help us understand "the gifts of God" in a broader sense which includes other blessings besides the Lord's Supper.[7] At the same time, however, I want to retain that note of expectancy which attends eucharistic worship. The people of God are always those who come to him in need, confident that he will satisfy and purify their desires with his abundant gifts.

Throughout our study I shall be using the terms "Pentecostal" and "neo-Pentecostal" as designations for contemporary groups of believers. Pentecostals are Christians who trace their theological lineage, and usually their denominational origins as well, back to an extraordinary revival that took place in Los Angeles at the

Azusa Street Church during the year 1906. Presiding over this multiracial event was a black pastor, W. J. Seymour. He had previously studied with a holiness minister named Charles F. Parham the Biblical evidence for a "third experience" of the Spirit beyond conversion and sanctification. The Azusa Street revival was characterized by a great outburst of speaking in tongues, some of which were understood by the participants to be actual foreign languages. Sympathetic visitors interpreted what was happening as a modern Pentecost, a second fulfillment of the risen Christ's prophecy in Acts 1:4f. that God's Spirit would descend upon his disciples with great power.[8] Seymour followed Luke and his teacher Parham in naming what the participants experienced a "baptism" in the Holy Spirit (see Acts 1:5; 2:1–4, 33; 10:44–47; 11: 15–17). With Parham he concluded that the necessary and sufficient evidence for having received it was glossolalia. Other charismatic gifts, such as healing and prophecy, also manifested themselves in the course of the year. Many who came as curious observers went away evangelists. The two largest Pentecostal denominations in the U.S.A. today—the Church of God in Christ and the Assemblies of God—both evolved from the Azusa Street revival.

The term "neo-Pentecostal" is harder to define since it does not generally appear as a self-designation. It may have been coined by journalists to denote members of the traditional denominations who have received the gift of tongues (and others) through a baptism in the Holy Spirit but who wish to remain affiliated with their parent churches. Such believers usually prefer to call themselves "charismatics" or "Spirit-filled Christians." Since we shall be building the case that all Christians ought to consider themselves charismatics, and further that the phrase "Spirit-filled" confuses more than it clarifies, I have decided to use "neo-Pentecostal," despite its origin outside the movement. No single event marks the beginning of the neo-Pentecostal movement, although the Spirit baptism experienced by Father Dennis Bennett at St. Mark's Episcopal Church, Van Nuys, California, in 1959 and the turmoil that resulted when members of the congregation took opposing views of their rector's charismatic leadership, is often cited as its first public surfacing.[9] Neo-Pentecostal believers now exist in practically every major U.S. denomination. Catholic neo-Pentecostals seem unusually visible within their church, in part no doubt because the hierarchy has generally taken a favorable view of their activity. Indeed, they number among their own at least one prince of the church: Léon Joseph Cardinal Suenens, Archbishop of Malines-Brussels.[10] As one might expect, neo-Pentecostal believers attempt to interpret their spiritual experience within the traditional teachings of their respective denominations whenever they can.

In closing this Introduction, I want to clarify my own stance as a Biblical interpreter and a believer. With regard to the former, I consider myself a practitioner of what is usually called historical-critical scholarship. This means, among other things, that when I look at a Biblical text, I want to learn first of all what its author wished to convey to the original readers. I try to carry out this enterprise, insofar as possible, without reference to what my denomination or any other theological tradition has said about the meaning of the text. In this way I hope to discover when contemporary church doctrine follows the ancient writer's intentions and when it departs from them. As a critical investigator I find myself convinced by the majority opinion of my colleagues that the traditions contained in the Old Testament have developed over the course of many centuries and do not necessarily represent a historically accurate record of the events reported. In the first instance they tell us what the final compiler of the traditions *believed* about these events.

As for the New Testament material, I take the position that Pauline disciples, not Paul himself, composed Ephesians, I and II Timothy, Titus, and (probably) Colossians.[11] These epistles obviously repeat many of Paul's ideas and may be based on some fragments of his genuine letters, but on the whole they reflect a period in church history subsequent to the apostle's death in the early 60's. Paul's real letters, written in the 50's, provide us with the oldest literary witness to Christian experience. Our four Gospels and Acts were written later, between A.D. 70 and 100. They naturally contain early traditions about Jesus and the young church, but it often becomes difficult to determine where this very old material leaves off and the author's interpretation of it begins. None of the Gospel writers claims to have been an eyewitness to Jesus' ministry. The anonymous author of the Third Gospel and Acts, called Luke in the church's tradition, may have been an occasional companion of Paul. The "we passages" in Acts (16: 10–17; 20:5–15; 21:1–18; 27:1 to 28:16), which narrate certain of the apostle's journeys in the first person plural, cover only a short span in his total ministry. Moreover, it has become clear in recent years that Luke is as much a preacher as a historian.[12] Thus, he sometimes idealizes his portrait of the early church for purposes of exhortation. As far as I can see, we have no reason to suspect that Luke *invented* the numerous stories he tells of charismatic phenomena in the early church. Paul's letters witness to the same widespread occurrence of charismata in his congregations. Nevertheless, we should be careful about assuming that everything happened just as Luke tells it, since he wrote some fifty years after Pentecost. We must also leave open the question of whether spiritual gifts formed a common part of the church's practice in his day. It is at least possible that he wrote his two-volume work to call the church of the 80's back to "the good old days." Therefore, although we must certainly regard Luke as an advocate of the charismata, Paul's writings furnish us with a more reliable guide to their actual practice in the early decades of the church's life.

As for my path within the Christian faith, I want to say simply that while I have never experienced anything so dramatic as a baptism in the Holy Spirit and I do not pray in tongues, God's guidance has sometimes been the most real thing in my life. Even from the standpoint of historical criticism I must conclude that the numerous reflections by New Testament writers upon the Spirit's work in their midst prove absolutely fundamental to their conceptualization of the gospel. By chance, disposition, or providence I count among my former parishioners and current friends many who could be called Pentecostals and neo-Pentecostals. Yet I resist joining their communities, for I find the theology and practice of both groups less than Biblical at certain key points. Nevertheless, this book will disappoint those who are looking for a harsh critique of the contemporary charismatic movements. I see it rather as an appeal for a Biblically honest theology of gifts. Frankly, I catch myself yearning for more of that deep joy and thankfulness which permeate the writings of the New Testament and sometimes get embodied in Pentecostal and neo-Pentecostal Christians today. In short, my answer to the question posed by the title of this Introduction is "Yes." I do see the appearance of charismata, whether ancient or modern, as a gracious challenge to the faith-lives of most traditional Christians, including my own. As I read it, the message disclosing itself to us in the gifts is this: "By the abundant grace of God, you can be more and do more according to his will than you presently think possible."

Every good and every perfect gift is from above and cometh down from the Father of lights, with whom is no variableness nor shadow of turning [James 1:17]. These words are so beautiful, so eloquent, so moving; they are so soothing and so comforting, so simple and comprehensible, so refreshing and so healing. Therefore we will beseech Thee, O God, that Thou wilt make the ears of those who hitherto have not regarded them, willing to accept them; that Thou wilt heal the misunderstanding heart by the understanding of the word, to understand the word; that Thou wilt incline the erring thought under the saving obedience of the word; that Thou wilt give the penitent soul confidence to dare to understand the word; and that Thou wilt make those who have understood it, more and more blessed therein, so that they may repeatedly understand it.

Amen.

Søren Kierkegaard,
from *Two Edifying Discourses* (1843)

CHAPTER 1

Common and Special Gifts in the Old Testament

A truly Biblical perspective on God's gifts to his people must begin with the ancient Hebrews. This is so for two reasons. First, though the New Testament writers were naturally subject to non-Hebraic influences from the Greek-speaking culture that surrounded them, their most profound heritage was that of Israel, contained in the Old Testament. The Greek Old Testament, or Septuagint, was the Bible most often used by the earliest Christians. More than any other resource, this book helped them interpret and express the new era inaugurated by Jesus. Almost all the great words of the New Testament—mercy, judgment, sin, grace, covenant, Christ—have an Israelite history. We do not properly understand what the New Testament writers were trying to communicate unless we know something of that history. We may say that the Old Testament has been fulfilled in the New, but that hardly means we can do away with the Old. The Gospel writers and Paul assumed that their readers were well versed in the Septuagint. They could not have imagined Christians trying to understand their words outside the context of Israel's scriptures.

This leads us to the second reason for beginning to paint our picture of God's gifts with the bold colors of the Old Testament. Because the New Testament writers gazed so intently upon the newness of Christ, they did not attempt to repeat everything God had revealed to them through the Old Testament. The New Testament makes no claim to being the *whole* counsel of God. Its writers assume that it will be supplemented in the readers' minds with

God's ancient wisdom. That is one reason why the Psalms found such ready acceptance in early Christian worship, despite the fact that the first believers also wrote their own songs (see Eph. 5:19f.).[1] For them the Old proved essential in comprehending the New. We too shall discover that New Testament thinking about God's gifts, rich as it is, needs the earthy teachings of the Old Testament.

Creation: God's Gift to All Humanity

Every ancient Hebrew would have agreed that without God there could be no world, no life. Selected verses from Psalm 104 express this conviction most beautifully:

> O LORD my God, thou art very great!
> Thou art clothed with honor and majesty,
>   who coverest thyself with light as with a
>   garment,
> who hast stretched out the heavens like a tent,
>   . . . .
> Thou dost cause the grass to grow for the cattle,
>   and plants for man to cultivate,
> that he may bring forth food from the earth,
>   and wine to gladden the heart of man,
> oil to make his face shine,
>   and bread to strengthen man's heart.
>   . . . .
> Thou hast made the moon to mark the seasons;
>   the sun knows its time for setting.
> Thou makest darkness, and it is night,
>   when all the beasts of the forest creep forth.
> The young lions roar for their prey,
>   seeking their food from God.
>   . . . .
> O LORD, how manifold are thy works!
>   . . . .
> Yonder is the sea, great and wide,
>   which teems with things innumerable,

> living things both small and great.
> There go the ships,
>> and Leviathan which thou didst form to sport
>> in it.
>
> These all look to thee,
>> to give them their food in due season.
> When thou givest to them, they gather it up;
>> when thou openest thy hand, they are filled
>> with good things.
> When thou hidest thy face, they are dismayed;
>> when thou takest away their breath, they die
>> and return to their dust.
> When thou sendest forth thy Spirit, they are
>> created;
>> and thou renewest the face of the ground.
>> (Ps. 104:1–2, 14–15, 19–21, 24, 25–30)

Psalm 104 describes what theologians have called *creatio continua,* continuous creation. As much as the ancient Hebrews valued God's rules and commandments for the ordering of the universe, they never saw these as substitutes for God's constant activity. His incessant caring, sustaining, and giving kept his world going. We do well to notice how many of the verbs in Psalm 104 are in the present tense and the active voice. God's world does not run on impersonal laws. He himself must be present to grow grass and plants, cover the earth with darkness, feed all living things, and, above all, grant us the breath of life. Here we encounter for the first time a truth that surfaces again and again in the Biblical record: divine gifts cannot be separated from their Giver. They are the gifts of *God,* or better, the daily giving of God. God alone is the source of our life; it is not anything we possess or produce.

Significantly, God's continuous creation appears in Psalm 104 as a *spiritual* activity. This recalls Gen. 1:1f., where the writer tells us that it was God's Spirit which moved over the primordial waters to create heaven and earth. Also, in Gen. 2:7 we find recorded that "the LORD God formed man of dust from the ground and breathed into his nostrils the breath [or spirit] of life." When the prophet

Isaiah looks forward to a glorious future time during which God will reestablish exiled Israel in its native land, he sees a vision of creation renewed by the Spirit:

> For the palace will be forsaken,
>   the populous city deserted;
> the hill and the watchtower
>   will become dens for ever,
> a joy of wild asses,
>   a pasture of flocks;
> until the Spirit is poured upon us from on high,
>   and the wilderness becomes a fruitful field,
>   and the fruitful field is deemed a forest.
>
> (Isa. 32:14f.)

The ancient Hebrews never separated the physical from the spiritual. What we call commonplace and ordinary (the growing of grass!) was for them holy, "charged with the grandeur of God."[2] This does not mean that the Hebrews were pantheists who identified God with the processes of nature. Far from it! Yet precisely because the Old Testament writers had discovered God's saving mercy and responded to it in obedience, they found their vision enlarged to comprehend the cosmic extent of his power. It was their God who held the whole world in his hand; the very air glowed with his presence. Old Testament writers did not trouble themselves with what we twentieth-century folk experience as a split between the material (or "scientific") and the supernatural. For them, there were no natural processes, no features of creation cut off from God's sustaining and renewing Spirit (Ps. 139:7–12). The psalmist expressed amazement that God should single out humankind as special recipients of his daily, extraordinary blessings:

> When I look at thy heavens, the work of thy fingers,
>   the moon and the stars which thou hast established;
> what is man that thou art mindful of him,
>   and the son of man that thou dost care for him?
>
> Yet thou hast made him little less than God,
>   and dost crown him with glory and honor.

> Thou hast given him dominion over the works of
>   thy hands;
>   thou hast put all things under his feet,
> all sheep and oxen,
>   and also the beasts of the field,
> the birds of the air, and the fish of the sea,
>   whatever passes along the paths of the sea.
>   (Ps. 8:3–8)

For such blessings, one can only praise him: "O LORD, our Lord, how majestic is thy name in all the earth!" (Ps. 8:9). It may be that those of us who seek "spiritual" gifts today should start with this elementary act of thankful awe in the presence of what we can see and taste and smell and feel of God's creation. According to the Old Testament, matter, when acknowledged as God's matter, becomes spiritual.

God's Special Gifts to Israel

As far as the blessings of creation are concerned, the Hebrews might be classified as universalists. For them, creation grace was "common." This did not mean cheap, but available to all. God's Spirit upholds every life (Job 33:4; 34:14), whether Israelite or not. To all nations he gives the gift of commerce (Eccl. 3:10). For all he numbers and names the stars (Ps. 147:4). Nevertheless, Israel came to know that it had received additional blessings—particular gifts—which marked it off from the rest of the earth's peoples for unusual privileges and responsibilities. Indeed, this reception of special gifts from God was what gave Israel its status as the people of God. God's gifts confer identity—a thought worth remembering as we try to discover who *we* are in this complex world! Foremost among Israel's special gifts was the promise made to Abraham and repeated, with modifications, down through the annals of Hebrew history. In the first statement of the promise God says to Abram:

> Go from your country and your kindred and your father's house to
> the land that I will show you. And I will make of you a great nation,
> and I will bless you, and make your name great, so that you will
> be a blessing. I will bless those who bless you, and him who curses

you I will curse; and by you all the families of the earth shall bless themselves. (Gen. 12:1–3)

But in this foundational story we recognize a paradox. For the very gift which granted Israel's uniqueness, which distinguished it from the world, was given *for the sake of the world.* Here a pattern emerges that repeats itself in various forms throughout the Old Testament and comes to a climax in the New Testament. God "restricts" his blessing by bestowing it upon only one person or a small group of people. But his whole purpose in doing so is to expand the blessing so that many, eventually all, will participate in it. Abram is a solitary individual, yet by him "all the families of the earth shall bless themselves." It is as if God's blessings must first appear in a limited and discriminatory guise before they can become universal. We do not know why God chose Abram. We find no hint in the text that he was seeking God at the time of his call or exhibited unusual moral qualifications for the job of promise bearer. Genesis 12:1ff. is one of many indications that God considers himself sovereignly free to give what he chooses when he chooses to whom he chooses, without regard to human merit (see Rom. 9:8–18).

God's manner of transmitting his promise sometimes appears altogether arbitrary. For example, in the story of Abraham's grandsons, Esau and Jacob, it is the younger man, Jacob, who, by trickery and in defiance of all ancient Near Eastern morality, extorts the birthright from his father and becomes the bearer of the promise (Gen., chs. 25 to 27). Jacob is a rascal and a deceiver, but because God's choice rests upon him from birth (Gen. 25:23) he prospers and becomes Israel, father of the twelve Hebrew tribes (Gen., ch. 49). God's inscrutable promise-fulfilling activity, not human faithfulness, calls the nation of Israel into being and showers special gifts upon it.

Gifts do follow, in abundance. When the descendants of Jacob fall into slavery in Egypt, God remembers his covenant with Abraham, Isaac, and Jacob (Ex. 2:23f.) and moves to deliver them through a series of extraordinary acts. The greatest of these was the miraculous salvation of the Hebrews from Pharaoh's army at the Reed Sea. This gift *par excellence* lives on in Israel's memory to the present moment as the supreme prototype of God's redemptive mercy. In the desert wanderings following this miracle God hosts his people with water and manna. Eventually, at Sinai, he establishes a covenant with them and grants them commandments to help them live out their chosenness, their holy separateness in the midst of the nations. For Israel's sake God sanctifies the seventh day as the Sabbath and presents it to his people as a gift (Ex. 16: 29). For Israel, God creates the priesthood from Aaron's family to aid the nation in its worship:

> Behold, I have taken your brethren the Levites from among the people of Israel; they are a gift to you, given to the LORD, to do the service of the tent of meeting. (Num. 18:6)

For Israel, God fashions a special benediction that has survived the centuries to refresh our spirits even today:

> The LORD bless you and keep you:
> The LORD make his face to shine
>   upon you, and be gracious to you:
> The LORD lift up his countenance
>   upon you, and give you peace.
>   (Num. 6:24–26)

All these gifts of election are corporate in nature. They belong to Israel as a whole, not to individuals. They constitute Israel's identity as chosen people of God, and though they may suffer misuse, they can never be revoked. For this reason Paul stands in awe of the Jews as God's gift bearers:

> They are Israelites, and to them belong the sonship, the glory, the covenants, the giving of the law, the worship, and the promises; to them belong the patriarchs, and of their race, according to the flesh, is the Christ. (Rom. 9:4f.)

Two chapters later Paul writes even more boldly to his Gentile readers on behalf of the Jews:

As regards the gospel they are enemies of God, for your sake; but
as regards election they are beloved for the sake of their forefathers.
For the gifts and the call of God are irrevocable. (Rom. 11:28f.)

The Greek word that Paul uses for "gifts" in this last verse is
charismata. That is hardly a slip of the apostolic pen, so it should
make us think twice when we feel tempted to restrict "spiritual"
gifts to Christian believers. Israel too must be seen as a charismatic
people, down to this very day.

After Israel's wilderness period God begins to fulfill the penulti-
mate part of his promise to Abraham: he leads Israel into the Holy
Land. Yet this fulfillment does not bring utopia. After a short
period of victorious celebration, Israel's loyalty to God crumbles.
Many begin to worship pagan deities. Again and again part or all
of Israel falls under the domain of a foreign power. God sends
strong prophets, judges, and kings to draw his people back to him,
but their response is at best ambivalent. Abraham's descendants no
longer look like a people through whom "all the families of the
earth shall bless themselves" (Gen. 12:3). Eventually most of the
inhabitants of the land are forced into exile in Babylon. There,
during a time of prolonged desolation, Israel begins to ponder the
reverse side of its blessings, namely, its calling, task, and mission
in the world. The postexilic prophet whom we call Second Isaiah
(Isa., chs. 40 to 66) expresses this growing sense of responsibility
most eloquently in the so-called "servant songs." In these poignant
verses the chosen people are assigned the role of God's suffering
servant. Here Israel thinks not about gifts of privilege but about
gifts of service (see especially Isa. 42:1–7). Israel, the bearer of
God's gifts, now receives a vocation to become God's gift for the
salvation of the nations. With this noble vision the last part of the
promise made to Abraham edges toward fulfillment.

Israel finds its identity and its task in its many gifts. But, as
always, the fundamental gift is the presence of God himself: "With
thee is the fountain of life" (Ps. 36:9). God makes promises and
bestows blessings, but his most gracious act is to accompany his
people. Above all, God walks "with" Israel. He speaks to the
patriarchs, prophets, and kings. He shepherds his people on the

wilderness march as a pillar of cloud by day, as a pillar of fire by night. He fights alongside Israel's armies. His glory inhabits the Tent of Meeting and later the Temple. When Israel reviews its history, it finds its greatest delight not in the numerous blessings that have flowed from its election by God, but in that election itself, in God's will to be near Israel:

> For the LORD has chosen Zion;
>> he has desired it for his habitation:
> "This is my resting place for ever;
>> here I will dwell, for I have desired it."
>> (Ps. 132:13f.)

The Lord has a passion to dwell among his people. That is the finest gift of all.

God's Charismatic Servants in Israel

Israel as a nation received gifts of election from God. But we also learn of individuals within Israel whom God singled out as special recipients of his Spirit. Ordinarily, the gift of God's Spirit raised up such people for the purpose of enlightening or liberating Israel. Let us risk a bit of confusion by employing the term "charismatic" to describe these Old Testament servants, despite the fact that no such word (or even equivalent word) exists in the Hebrew language. If, however, we understand the word to describe a person whose particular reception of God's Spirit differentiates him or her from other members of the community—and this is at least part of what the Greek word *charisma* means in the New Testament— we have sufficient reason for applying it to those ancient Israelites with whom the *ruach* of God dwelt or upon whom it fell.

Some of these charismatic figures in Israel's history received the Spirit only temporarily or for only one specific task. They are remembered for their Spirit-empowered deeds, but for nothing else. Among such people were the seventy elders of Israel who prophesied around the Tabernacle in the wilderness because God had placed upon them "some" of the Spirit which rested on Moses. This prophesying lasted only a short time (Num. 11:16f., 24f.).

Curiously, "exceptions" always mark the movement of God's Spirit. Two elders named Eldad and Medad, who were not among the seventy chosen by Moses to accompany him to the Tabernacle, nevertheless received the Spirit and began to prophesy. This irregularity disturbed Moses' lieutenant, Joshua, so he asked his master to silence the two. But Moses replied (prophetically):

> Are you jealous for my sake? Would that all the LORD's people were prophets, that the LORD would put his spirit upon them! (Num. 11: 29)

Others upon whom the Spirit seems to have alighted only fleetingly are the obscure judges Othniel (Judg. 3:9–11) and Jephthah (Judg. 11:29–32). Their single "spiritual" task was to lead Israel in battle against the oppressors under whom it had fallen after its first conquest of the land. According to Ex. 31:2ff., God chose Bezalel the craftsman and filled him with the Spirit to direct the construction of the Tabernacle and the Ark. We do not learn what effect, if any, this gift had on his private life. Nor do we know how long it lasted. We may guess, however, that it was a "functional" gift, temporarily enjoyed. Much later in Israel's history, when David defied King Saul by gathering about himself a band of rebel soldiers, Amasai, a defector from Saul's army, swore loyalty to David with an oath inspired by the Spirit (I Chron. 12:16–18). We never hear of him again. Equally transient are Azariah (II Chron. 15: 1ff.), Jahaziel (II Chron. 20:13ff.), and Zechariah (II Chron. 24: 20ff.), each of whom arose to speak a single prophecy in the Spirit. As soon as they accomplish their tasks, they vanish from the Biblical record. "The wind blows where it wills, and you hear the sound of it, but you do not know whence it comes or whither it goes." (John 3:8.)

On the other hand, the Old Testament also tells us of charismatic figures in whom the Spirit dwelt or upon whom it rested. There is a note of permanence, or at least regularity, about the Spirit's presence in their lives. Surprisingly, the patriarchs Abraham, Isaac, and Jacob, though extraordinarily gifted by God, were not identified as charismatics by the Biblical authors. God remained with them, but the Spirit is never said to be in or upon them. Joseph, son of Jacob, seems to have been the first Hebrew charismatic. With God's help he accurately interpreted Pharaoh's dream. The grateful Egyptian monarch then established Joseph as his high chamberlain, having discerned in him an unusual measure of the divine Spirit. (Gen. 41:38–40.) A similar recognition of charismatic wisdom in an Israelite occurs when the Babylonian King Nebuchadnezzar praises Daniel as a dream interpreter and wise man without peer "in whom is the spirit of the holy gods [or God]" (Dan. 4:8ff., 18; see also 5:11–16).

According to the Old Testament witness as a whole, Israel's foremost charismatic leader was Moses. Little is actually said about Moses' relationship to the Spirit. We learn only that some of the Spirit which remained upon him found its way to the seventy elders (Num. 11:24f.) and that he himself transmitted the "spirit of wisdom" to Joshua by the laying on of hands (Deut. 34:9). Yet the authors of the Pentateuch clearly regard Moses as God's most powerful servant. God chose him and remained with him in a singular way (see Ex., ch. 3). No ancient Hebrew could match him in gifts. Of him the Deuteronomist wrote:

> And there has not arisen a prophet since in Israel like Moses, whom the LORD knew face to face, none like him for all the signs and the wonders which the LORD sent him to do in the land of Egypt, ... and for all the mighty power and all the great and terrible deeds which Moses wrought in the sight of all Israel. (Deut. 34:10–12)

Moses' servant and immediate successor, Joshua, also emerges in the Biblical record as a "long-term" charismatic. According to tradition, he enjoyed this blessing even before he received the call to take his master's place. Toward the end of Moses' career God commanded the lawgiver:

> Take Joshua, the son of Nun, a man in whom is the spirit, and lay your hand upon him; cause him to stand before Eleazar the priest and all the congregation, and you shall commission him in their sight. You shall invest him with some of your authority, that all the congregation of the people of Israel may obey. (Num. 27:18–20)

After Moses' death, Joshua received a personal promise from God: "As I was with Moses, so I will be with you" (Josh. 1:5). Yet, as in Moses' case, we cannot tell from the text when or how the Spirit entered him.

Gideon and Samson were two remarkable men from the period of Israel's judges. Like Moses and Joshua, Gideon received the promise that the Lord was with him (Judg. 6:12). God confirmed his presence in a charismatic way when "the Spirit of the LORD took possession of Gideon" to raise him up as a general who would lead Israel against the Midianites and Amalekites (Judg. 6:33ff.). Samson seems to have been stirred by the Spirit from his boyhood (Judg. 13:25). One gets the impression that both he and Gideon experienced God's presence in a way that the other judges did not. Significantly, however, the texts never say that the Spirit dwelt in them or rested on them. Rather, it came upon them periodically and mightily to take control of them (Judg. 6:34f.; 14:6, 19; 15:14f.; 16:28). In this respect they seem different from charismatic leaders such as Joseph, Moses, Joshua, and Daniel. The Spirit remained with the latter; apparently, it did not "seize" them ecstatically.

Saul and David can also qualify as charismatics. Each was anointed king of Israel by the prophet Samuel (with whom, for all his clairvoyant power and intimacy with God, the Biblical text never associates the Spirit!). Shortly after his anointing, Saul met a band of prophets and, just as Samuel had predicted, "the Spirit of God came mightily upon him, and he prophesied among them" (I Sam. 10:10). Presumably, this was an ecstatic experience, for Samuel had foretold that through it Saul would "be turned into another man" (I Sam. 10:6). In the knowledge that God favored him (I Sam. 10:7) and by means of Samuel's aid, Saul established himself on the throne. As long as he pleased God, the Spirit remained upon him. But when he failed to fulfill a divine command (I Sam., ch. 15), David was chosen king in his place. Immediately after David received his anointing for office, the Spirit "came mightily upon [him] from that day forward" (I Sam. 16:13). But concerning Saul, the court historian reports that "the Spirit of the LORD departed from Saul, and an evil spirit from the LORD tormented him" (I Sam. 16:14). Here disobedience brings about "despiritualization." Meanwhile, the Spirit worked wondrous effects upon David. Though a mere youth, he soon became "skilful in playing [the lyre], a man of valor, a man of war, prudent in speech, and a man of good presence; and the LORD [was] with him" (I Sam. 16:18). Later, when David sinned with Bathsheba, he feared that God would withdraw his presence as he had done from Saul. This is the interpretation that the compiler of the psaltery placed upon Psalm 51, which he entitled "A Psalm of David, when Nathan the prophet came to him, after he had gone in to Bathsheba." In vs. 10f. of the psalm we find the well-known words:

> Create in me a clean heart, O God,
>   and put a new and right spirit within me.
> Cast me not away from thy presence,
>   and take not thy holy Spirit from me.
>   (Ps. 51:10f.)

Here David acknowledges that the renewal of his spirit depends upon the continuing presence of God's Spirit. The prayer received a positive answer. David suffered for his sin, but the court history in II Samuel and I Kings gives no indication that God's Spirit ever departed from him.

Israel's prophets are said to have spoken their words by God's Spirit (Neh. 9:30; Zech. 7:12), though they do not often acknowledge the Spirit's influence explicitly in their writings. Second Isaiah (Isa. 61:1) and Micah (Micah 3:8) mention the Spirit's guidance, and Ezekiel reports frequent experiences of being entered (Ezek. 2: 2; 3:24) or lifted up (Ezek. 3:14; 8:3; etc.) by the Spirit. Sometimes God's *ruach* even transports him from Babylon to Jerusalem and back. Apart from these references, however, the literary prophets of the Old Testament do not connect the Spirit directly with their work. On the other hand, Elijah and Elisha, who apparently did not write books, clearly functioned as charismatic prophets. It was reported of Elijah that the Spirit of the Lord carried him about (I Kings 18:12). Presumably, the Spirit stayed with him more or less continuously, for his disciple Elisha noticed an extraordinary quality about him and therefore asked for a "double portion" of his spirit (II Kings 2:9ff.). Elisha's request was granted (although we are never sure whether he received the desired quantity!). Moreover, his gift found certification when the school of prophets at Jericho recognized him as their master's legitimate successor. Bowing down to the ground before him, they exclaimed, "The spirit of Elijah rests upon Elisha" (II Kings 2:15).[3]

Our picture of God's charismatic servants in Israel would not be complete without a glance toward the future as envisioned by the Old Testament writers. The most illustrious of all God's servants who would bear his Spirit in the coming time of renewal was, of course, the Messiah. Only one Old Testament passage clearly links the Messiah with the Spirit, but it is a passage that has etched its way deep into the consciousness of Jews and Christians alike:

> There shall come forth a shoot from the stump of Jesse,
>   and a branch shall grow out of his roots.
> And the Spirit of the LORD shall rest upon him,
>   the spirit of wisdom and understanding,
>   the spirit of counsel and might,
>   the spirit of knowledge and the fear of the LORD.
> And his delight shall be in the fear of the LORD.
>
> (Isa. 11:1–3)

But if the Messiah was to be granted the perpetual gift of the Spirit, the people of Israel too could hope for a share in this abundance. In Second Isaiah, God speaks this promise:

> Behold my servant, whom I uphold,
>   my chosen, in whom my soul delights;
> I have put my spirit upon him,
>   he will bring forth justice to the nations.
>
> (Isa. 42:1)

If we are right in understanding the servant in this passage as Israel (see Isa. 49:3), then the prophet looks forward to a time when all of God's people will become charismatics. In the Spirit they will find power for their task of bringing righteousness to the world. This vision fits well with another passage in Second Isaiah in which God promises to pour his Spirit upon the descendants of his servant Jacob (Isa. 44:1–3). It also coheres with hopes expressed by two other prophets who wrote late in Israel's history. According to Ezekiel, prophesying in Babylon, God will bless his people with a new heart and a new spirit upon their return from exile. Indeed, he will put his own Spirit within them so that they can walk willingly according to his commandments (Ezek. 11:19; 18:31; 37:14; 39:29; and especially 36:26f.). In the prophecy of Joel, written sometime after the Babylonian exile, God vows that

> . . . afterward . . . I will pour out my spirit on all flesh;
> your sons and your daughters shall prophesy,
>   your old men shall dream dreams,
>   and your young men shall see visions.
> Even upon the menservants and maidservants
>   in those days, I will pour out my spirit.
>
> (Joel 2:28f.)

This word of the Lord seems to resonate with Moses' wish that all God's people might become prophets (Num. 11:29). Students of the New Testament will recall that it is this text from Joel which forms the center of Peter's Pentecost sermon in Acts 2:16ff. Thus, particularly in the later writings of the Old Testament, prophets begin to envision the messianic age as an era when spiritual gifts heretofore bestowed upon only a few individuals will be poured out upon the whole nation of Israel.

The Ezekiel passages that link the gift of the Spirit with obedience must be highlighted at this point in our discussion, for, understood within the context of Judaism in Jesus' day, they prove more radical than they seem. Ezekiel hears God saying:

> A new heart I will give you, and a new spirit I will put within you; and I will take out of your flesh the heart of stone and give you a heart of flesh. And I will put my spirit within you, and cause you to walk in my statutes and be careful to observe my ordinances. (Ezek. 36:26f.)

This passage suggests that the purpose of God's charismatic gift in the latter days is to sanctify. The inner life of God's people will be transformed so that they may obey him naturally, without great effort. The external written law, beloved by Judaism as God's supreme gift, will become unnecessary! Only the forward-looking sections of Isaiah (Isa. 11:1–3; 42:1f.; 61:1ff.) approach Ezekiel's vision of a transformed people. This may surprise us, for the New

Testament writers take it for granted that one of the Spirit's chief roles is that of Sanctifier (see, for example, I Cor. 14:1ff.; Gal. 5: 16–25; Rom. 8:1–11).

It might be argued that in the Old Testament, God's Spirit always accomplishes his will and therefore, inevitably, sanctifies. Ultimately, this stance proves correct. Yet if we review the stories of God's charismatic servants in Israel, we find that by New Testament standards many of them were less than sterling characters. Gideon was moved by God's Spirit to become a mighty warrior, but he remained a vain and half-believing man who kept many wives and eventually combined his devotion to God with worship of a golden vestment (Judg. 6:11 to 8:32). Immediately after receiving the Spirit, the judge Jephthah foolishly vowed that if he emerged victorious over the Ammonites, he would sacrifice up to the Lord as a burnt offering the first person who came out of his house to meet him. The victim was none other than his daughter (Judg. 11:29–40). Samson the strong man came out weak on maturity. Though the Spirit of the Lord had stirred him since his childhood (Judg. 13:25), he remained a lifelong adolescent. He married a pagan wife, taunted people with lies and riddles that caused great loss of innocent life, visited prostitutes, and generally multiplied hatred between Israel and the Philistines (Judg., chs. 14 to 16).

Saul, who had been "turned into another man" through his ecstatic experience of the Spirit (I Sam., ch. 10), nevertheless disobeyed a clear command of the Lord (I Sam., ch. 15) and lost God's favor. David, who apparently enjoyed an even greater measure of the Spirit, descended to adultery and murder. Elisha the prophet received a double measure of Elijah's spirit, but he was hardly an amiable fellow, as the following story shows:

> He went up . . . to Bethel; and while he was going up on the way, some small boys came out of the city and jeered at him, saying, "Go up, you baldhead! Go up, you baldhead!" And he turned around, and when he saw them, he cursed them in the name of the LORD. And two she-bears came out of the woods and tore forty-two of the boys. (II Kings 2:23f.)

God's Spirit accomplished his purposes by taking over the lives of individuals. But it did not necessarily sanctify the lives of its recipients—nor did it always bring them into a positive fellowship with God.

Two stories illustrate this latter point. According to Num., chs. 22 to 24, Balak, king of the Moabites, engaged the mercenary prophet Balaam to curse Israel. But when non-Israelite Balaam attempted to fulfill his end of the contract, God intervened and repeatedly prevented him from speaking a bad word against the chosen people. Finally the Spirit of God came upon him and inspired him to speak a great blessing over Israel (Num. 24:2ff.). Yet when the whole event came to an end, Balaam simply went home, presumably neither worse nor better than before. Apparently he remained a pagan. The Spirit had momentarily possessed, but not transformed him.

Our second story concerns King Saul, whom God's Spirit had forsaken following his act of disobedience (I Sam. 16:14). Saul hated and feared David, knowing that God's blessing had now fallen upon his young rival. When the king learned that David was hiding with Samuel in Ramah, he sent messengers to seize and kill him. But when the messengers arrived and saw Samuel's associates prophesying before him, they themselves fell under the Spirit's power. They too began to prophesy ecstatically and thus found themselves incapable of carrying out their mission. The same thing happened with a second and third group of messengers (I Sam. 19: 18–20). Finally, in desperation, Saul decided to go to Ramah and capture David himself.

> And he went . . . to Naioth in Ramah; and the Spirit of God came upon him also, and as he went he prophesied, until he came to Naioth in Ramah. And he too stripped off his clothes, and he too prophesied before Samuel, and lay naked all that day and all that night. Hence it is said, "Is Saul also among the prophets?" (I Sam. 19:23f.)

Saul became immobilized but not sanctified. For the rest of his life he remained alienated from David and God. These comic-tragic stories reveal something mysterious about God's Spirit in the Old

Testament which is not easily dovetailed with the New Testament understanding of the Spirit as the One who inspires new birth (John 3:3ff.), as the supreme source of "love, joy, peace, patience, kindness, goodness, faithfulness, gentleness, and self-control" (Gal. 5: 22f.).

Other questions pertaining to the Old Testament view of the Spirit are also worth pondering. How does the Spirit come? Can we find a degree of consistency in its advent? The Spirit's violent arrival seems well documented. Sometimes, as with the judges, certain of the prophets, and Saul, it overpowers people and takes possession of them to accomplish God's purpose. The Hebrew words used to describe this sort of coming are *tsalach,* meaning "penetrate" or "rush upon" (Judg. 14:6, 19; 15:14; I Sam. 10:10), and *labash,* which literally means "to clothe oneself with" (Judg. 6:34; I Chron. 12:18; II Chron. 24:20). But a subtler, more gradual coming seems hinted at in Judg. 13:24f. where the writer notes that God's Spirit "began to stir" Samson in his boyhood. And how did the Spirit fill Bezalel, the craftsman who designed the Tabernacle and the Ark? Perhaps it came through visions, but certainly not in any way that prevented him from communicating with his fellow workmen. As for the manner in which God's Spirit first appeared in the lives of charismatic figures such as Joseph, Moses, and Daniel, who seem to have maintained almost constant contact with it, the Old Testament remains silent. All we get is the impression that the Spirit somehow lingered so close to these people that periodic overpowerings proved unnecessary. Joshua received the "spirit of wisdom" from Moses by the laying on of hands (Deut. 34:9), but this happened after the Spirit had already dwelt within him for some time (Num. 27:18–20). At neither stage of Joshua's life are we informed of his inner experience. We must conclude, then, that in the Old Testament, God's Spirit visited people in a variety of ways. The only constant feature of its coming, clearly a most important one, is that no one could prepare for its arrival. Except for Elisha, who desired a double portion of Elijah's spirit, no individual in the Old Testament sought or claimed the Spirit's presence. And even in Elisha's case its advent is best understood as an act of God's sovereign freedom.

Gifts Contingent and Unconditional

We can clarify our understanding of what God's gifts meant to the ancient Hebrews if we notice that all of them, whether explicitly linked with the Spirit or not, fall into one of two categories. Either they come for particular well-defined purposes, i.e., with specified conditions, or they are given freely with no preparation or prescription for use, with no strings attached.

Samson's strength and the repeated visitations of the Spirit which stirred it up belong to the first category. The gifts bestowed upon Samson come as the result of a promise made to his mother through the angel of the Lord:

> Behold, you are barren and have no children; but you shall conceive and bear a son. Therefore beware, and drink no wine or strong drink, and eat nothing unclean, for lo, you shall conceive and bear a son. No razor shall come upon his head, for the boy shall be a Nazirite to God from birth; and he shall begin to deliver Israel from the hand of the Philistines. (Judg. 13:3–5)

Samson's gifts are contingent in two ways. They depend upon his remaining a Nazirite, and they must function to deliver Israel. Presumably, it is because he allows himself to suffer the loss of his Nazirite status (by revealing his vulnerability to Delilah) and because he neglects his mission to liberate Israel that God departs from him (Judg. 16:20). When his strength returns for one last moment to bring the temple of Dagon crashing down upon his Philistine captors, it comes in response to his prayer. Samson cries out:

> O Lord GOD, remember me, I pray thee, and strengthen me, I pray thee, only this once, O God, that I may be avenged upon the Philistines for one of my two eyes. (Judg. 16:28)

Samson's prayer may strike us as terribly vindictive, but by the standards of the day it was also repentant: Samson was now remembering his mission and desiring to fulfill it. Samson's story shows that gifts can be lost through unfaithfulness but regained through seeking—if that seeking coincides with God's purposes.

The kingship and attendant blessings of the Spirit given to Saul also manifest contingency. When Saul failed to fulfill God's command to destroy the Amalekites utterly, he saw his gifts recalled. The Biblical text puts it bluntly:

> And the LORD repented that he had made Saul king over Israel. (I Sam. 15:35)

> Now the Spirit of the LORD departed from Saul, and an evil spirit from the LORD tormented him. (I Sam. 16:14)

Like Samson, Saul repented of his disobedience (I Sam. 15:24ff.). As a result, he received permission to worship God with Samuel one last time (I Sam. 15:35), and his reign was allowed to continue for some years. Although God's favor had departed from him, he held some residual power by virtue of his anointing for office. The effects of God's choice did not pass away immediately. Nevertheless, without God's gracious presence Saul became a sad and contradictory man whose demise can only be called tragic (I Sam., ch. 31). After his sin the Spirit of God came upon him only once more, and then (we have noted above) not as a blessing but as a humiliating deterrent to his evil intentions toward David.

Some gifts therefore prove contingent because one may lose them through misuse. The contingency of others consists in the fact that one appropriates them only with effort. When Jacob confronts a dark figure by the Jabbok River and wrestles with him all night, he virtually forces a gift from him: "I will not let you go unless you bless me" (Gen. 32:26). Jacob literally seizes this opportunity, for he senses that his opponent holds the power to bestow wonderous things. The man's identity is revealed in his gift to Jacob: "Your name shall no more be called Jacob, but Israel, for you have striven with God, and with men, and have prevailed" (Gen. 32:28). Jacob's "victory," however, comes at a price. He walks away from the struggle with a permanent limp (Gen. 32:25, 31f.). It seems that some of God's gifts must wound their recipients. We shall have more to say about this mystery in Chapter 5. Jacob did not initiate the momentous wrestling match recorded in Gen., ch. 32. It came upon him by God's fiat. But in the midst of the conflict he discerned that his opponent embodied some great blessing, so he fought like a bulldog to retain it. The story reveals that gifts sometimes come as a result of human struggle with God. Had Jacob let the angel go, the blessing might have eluded him.

Hannah, the barren woman who became Samuel's mother, did not confront a visible or tangible divine adversary. Her "opportunity" for contending with God was her own sorrow, her desolation over her childlessness. Though unjustly accused of drunkenness by the priest Eli, she persisted in her agitated prayer to God before the sanctuary at Shiloh, vowing that if the Lord should grant her a child, she would devote him to divine service as a Nazirite. According to the story, Hannah spoke to God out of her "great anxiety and vexation" (I Sam. 1:16). We should probably understand her words as an expression of anger against the God who, as the text says, "had closed her womb" (I Sam. 1:5f.). Out of her deep feeling she so protested her condition to God that Eli the priest felt moved to pronounce a blessing upon her. "Go in peace," he said, "and the God of Israel grant your petition which you have made to him." (I Sam. 1:17.) The text does not tell us specifically that Hannah's prayer and Eli's blessing changed God's mind, but that is surely the impression the text gives, for shortly afterward Hannah conceives and bears Samuel.[4] The gift of the child proves to be contingent in two ways: it comes through Hannah's seeking and with the condition that Samuel be devoted to God's service.

David's son Solomon also receives a contingent gift. When God appears to the young king in a dream and says to him, "Ask what I shall give you," Solomon must make a choice. He *will* be gifted, but his gifting requires decision and involves risk. He may choose foolishly or selfishly, so his future hangs in the balance. Solomon wisely requests "an understanding mind to govern thy people, that I may discern between good and evil; for who is able to govern this thy great people?" (I Kings 3:9). God takes pleasure in Solomon's appeal and responds with a great blessing:

> Because you have asked this, and have not asked for yourself long life or riches or the life of your enemies, but have asked for yourself

understanding to discern what is right, behold, I now do according to your word. Behold, I give you a wise and discerning mind, so that none like you has been before you and none like you shall arise after you. I give you also what you have not asked, both riches and honor, so that no other king shall compare with you, all your days. And if you will walk in my ways, keeping my statutes and my commandments, as your father David walked, then I will lengthen your days. (I Kings 3:11–14)

Solomon's wise choice has the effect of begetting further gifts. Because he seeks a gift for the chosen people rather than for himself, he is blessed beyond measure. God initiates the gift-giving process, but the substance of what the king receives depends, at least in part, upon how he chooses.

In the stories above, God's gifts come with conditions. Their reception or retention is somehow bound up with human activity. A gift is sought. In a moment of opportunity, itself given, a gift is grasped. Or, through wrong action, a gift is lost. One could almost conclude that there are ground rules for the proper reception and nurturing of God's gifts.

We find this supposition confirmed especially in the writings of the Deuteronomic historian. A dramatic recitation of "rules" takes place shortly after Israel enters the Promised Land. On Mt. Gerizim stand six of the twelve tribes of Israel to symbolize God's blessings; and on Mt. Ebal stand the other six tribes to embody the curses. Both blessings and cursings, spoken aloud by the Levites, are conditional. If Israel obeys God's commandments, the land will bring forth great harvest and the animals will multiply. But if Israel disobeys, God will send nothing but confusion, frustration, and destruction. (Deut., ch. 28.) In the Deuteronomic view similar blessings and cursings hang over Israel's kings (I Sam. 12:13–15) and its Temple (I Kings 9:1–9)—indeed, over all its institutions. Many of the prophets also echo the conviction that if Israel remains obedient to God's commands, God will multiply its blessings, but if Israel sins, he will cut off his gifts and send bad times.

This clear-cut system of rewards and punishments does not, however, prevail everywhere in the Old Testament. The Book of Job, for example, presents us with a monumental dissenting opinion, for it dares to ask why the righteous must suffer. Here we must also think of the frequent Old Testament assertions that God's good favor toward Israel's fathers and heroes will never depart. This view reveals itself with special clarity in the lives of Abraham, Jacob, and David. To Abraham, God makes a promise that will reach fulfillment quite apart from how eagerly or reluctantly the patriarch accepts it. Abraham *will* become father of many nations. All the nations of the earth *will* bless themselves in him. Even when Abraham doubts these promises or tries to take their fulfillment into his own hands, God refuses to cast him off. Similarly, once God chooses Jacob as the promise bearer, it does not matter that he defrauds his brother, Esau, or tricks his father-in-law, Laban. The blessing of God rests on him still, and he prospers. In his case too God's choice means unconditional good fortune. David suffers much for his sin with Bathsheba. Yet, like Jacob and unlike Saul, he never experiences final rejection by God. In fact, he receives a divine pledge which has continued to shape Israel's messianic expectations down to the present day. Through Nathan the prophet God promises nothing less than a perpetual throne for David's descendants.

> I will not take my steadfast love from [your offspring], as I took it from Saul, whom I put away from before you. And your house and your kingdom shall be made sure for ever before me; your throne shall be established for ever. (II Sam. 7:15f.)

It is easy to see why Israel's later prophets, and therefore the Jews of Jesus' day, would come to envision the Messiah as Son of David (see Isa. 11:1ff.; Jer. 33:14ff.; Micah 5:2; Zech., ch. 12). Only such a person could embody the fulfillment of this promise.

Because of God's gracious dealings with the promise bearers Abraham, Jacob, and David, not a few Old Testament writers celebrate the unconditional nature of God's "steadfast love" for the whole nation of Israel. These writers know, of course, that God punishes his people for their unfaithfulness to the conditional Sinai covenant. They see that he even allows them to languish in exile far from the Promised Land. David's royal line seems to disappear. Jerusalem falls, the Temple suffers destruction and the glory of the

Lord departs from it. Yet, somehow, the promises still stand. The Torah, with its stories and commandments, continues to reside with Israel, testifying to God's mercies. Thus, the postexilic writers are led to conclude that despite all appearances God's "steadfast love endures for ever" (Ps. 136; see also Ps. 103:8–10; Micah 7:19f.). Hopeless as things seem, God will stand by his promises to the fathers and continue to extend them to the whole nation.

The details of this grand vision are spelled out most powerfully by the prophets Jeremiah and Ezekiel. Jeremiah speaks of a future idyllic time when God will establish a "new covenant" with Israel. No longer will he set external commandments over them, with the condition that people must learn and obey these precepts in order to be blessed. In the coming days, God says:

> I will put my law within them, and I will write it upon their hearts; and I will be their God, and they shall be my people. And no longer shall each man teach his neighbor and each his brother, saying, "Know the LORD," for they shall all know me, from the least of them to the greatest. (Jer. 31:33f.)

Obedience itself will be the blessing, for walking in God's precepts will come as naturally as knowing one's own heart. While Jeremiah appears to distinguish the new covenant he describes from the Sinai covenant (Jer. 31:32), he sees it as entirely consistent with the promise made to David (Jer. 33:14–22). Ezekiel uses somewhat different language, but he seems to be pointing to the same future as his brother-prophet. He hears God saying to Israel:

> A new heart I will give you, and a new spirit I will put within you; and I will take out of your flesh the heart of stone and give you a heart of flesh. And I will put my spirit within you, and cause you to walk in my statutes and be careful to observe my ordinances. (Ezek. 36:26f.)

Here we are digging in familiar ground. We have examined this passage earlier in connection with Israel's hope for a bestowal of the Spirit upon all God's people. It is no accident that such a hope coincides with God's unconditional steadfast love. The prophet conceives of the Spirit and the new age it will inaugurate as blessings granted through God's free grace. Moreover, as in Jeremiah, this final gift coincides with the fulfillment of God's covenant with David (Ezek. 37:24ff.).

When the later Old Testament writers envision Israel's ideal future, they picture it to themselves in images from the past, yet without the defects of the past. Once God's great era has broken in, David's heir will reign in perfect righteousness. Obedience, once a burden, will be the same as free will. The Spirit, formerly given to only a few, will rest upon all God's people. No longer can the covenant be broken by rebellion or unfaithfulness. Then it will stand forever. All these blessings are God's unconditional gifts. Never again will he recall them.

Many mysteries remain with regard to the tension between contingent and unconditional gifts in the Old Testament. Perhaps we simply cannot know why some gifts are temporary or limited in scope, while others endure; why some gifts function like rewards, while others appear to be pure grace; why some recipients must seek, while others are sought; why some receive more blessings than others, even though they seem no more deserving; why some lose their gifts for comparatively minor sins, while others retain their gifts in spite of grave sins. The Old Testament refuses to present neat answers to these questions. Its authors show more interest in witnessing to the richness of Israel's giftedness, however diverse and paradoxical. And most of all they want to place us before the benevolent, terrible Giver of all gifts whose freedom to bestow in his own way we ignore at our peril: "I will be gracious to whom I will be gracious, and will show mercy to whom I will show mercy" (Ex. 33:19). He is the Lord, and with him is the fountain of life.

Some Conclusions

In order to understand God's common and special gifts in the Old Testament we have, somewhat anachronistically, marked out a category of people called "charismatics." These, we said, were persons whose gift of God's Spirit set them apart from the rest of Israel for special honors and/or tasks. Among such charismatics we found some of Israel's greatest heroes: Joseph, Moses, Joshua, Elijah, Elisha, David, and Daniel. With them, the Spirit or a spiritual gift resided more or less continuously. We also found lesser-known figures, persons upon whom the Spirit fell only temporarily to empower them for specific acts. To this group belong the seventy elders in the days of Moses, the judges Othniel and Jephthah, the soldier Amasai, and the prophetic figures Azariah, Jahaziel, and Zechariah. Further, we discovered that some charismatics in Israel deserve no commendation for their morality and faithfulness to God. Here we have in mind Gideon, Samson, Jephthah, Balaam, and Saul. While the gifts granted to these men differentiated them from their community by entrusting them with special powers, the Spirit did not sanctify them. On the other hand, we learned that several of Israel's most illustrious figures, such as Abraham, Isaac, Jacob, and Samuel, were never directly linked by the tradition with God's Spirit, despite the fact that they clearly lived on the most intimate terms with God and received extraordinary blessings from him. In short, not all of Israel's charismatics devoted themselves wholeheartedly to God, and not all of God's special favorites qualify as Spirit-filled people. This raises the question of how legitimate it is, in formulating our understanding of what the Old Testament means by gifts, to center our gaze on individuals blessed with a special measure of God's Spirit.

Two other pieces of data complicate the picture still further. First, the Old Testament writers sometimes view God's "continuing creation" of the material world as a work of the Spirit (Ps. 104: 27ff.; Isa. 32:14f.). This spiritual gift can be called "common," for it does not locate itself in specially chosen people but presents itself to the entire world. According to the author of Genesis, God's Spirit associates itself with *all* matter, not just the bodies of particular Israelites (Gen. 1:2). Second, Paul's designation of the gifts accompanying Israel's election as charismata (Rom. 11:29)[5] challenges us to expand our definition of "charismatic" to include phenomena not explicitly linked with the Spirit by the Old Testament writers. In summary, not every gift of the Spirit differentiates, and not every differentiating charisma is named in the tradition as a gift of the Spirit. The term "divine gift" seems far more useful in describing Israel's overall experience of God's blessings than "spiritual gift." Moreover, if Rom. 11:29 is at all typical, the former term may also prove more accurate in defining what the New Testament means by charisma. We shall test this hypothesis in Chapter 4. First we need to take a broad view of the New Testament's teaching about gifts.

CHAPTER 2

Giftedness in the New Testament Church

"You know the grace of our Lord Jesus Christ, that though he was rich, yet for your sake he became poor, so that by his poverty you might become rich." (II Cor. 8:9.) Paul's gemlike paradox states the theme of this chapter in concise form. In essence, it is that the New Testament was written by and for people who felt themselves extraordinarily gifted by God through the events surrounding the ministry of Jesus. Both authors and readers were convinced that they lived in days of great abundance. Moreover, New Testament believers generally expected that the abundance they were enjoying would soon be further multiplied. When Jesus Christ returned to rule over a transformed earth their blessings would extend beyond their most extravagant dreams.[1] Our objective in the present chapter is not simply to establish this thesis but, more importantly, to explore the wide range of experience and linguistic interpretations of experience which gave shape to the church's sense of giftedness. As we proceed with our study, it may profit us to ask ourselves how the life of the early Christian believers either confirms or challenges our own way of life. To what extent are we as gifted as they thought themselves to be?

The Emotions of Abundant Life

It would be quite wrong to suggest that the New Testament is all about sweetness and light. Unfortunately, some Christians today interpret it that way, thereby laying upon themselves and others the impossible burden of being constantly happy. I once watched powerless as a young woman slipped toward a nervous breakdown because she insisted on seeing nothing but Jesus' miraculous victories in her life and in the world around her. She could not allow herself to feel the deep pain of her own loneliness. Eventually her subconscious life caught up with her, and she had to be hospitalized until she learned to accept the facts of her alienation. The New Testament never insists that believers live in a state of constant euphoria. Its writers know much of suffering, anger, and even despair, and are literally candid about it. We shall reflect on how these dark corners of life fit together with the early church's sense of giftedness in Chapter 5.

Presently, however, we want to note that a large part of the New Testament *is* written out of a profound hopefulness about God's purposes for humankind. "I came," says the Johannine Jesus, "that [my sheep] may have life, and have it abundantly" (John 10:10). The aroma of celebration rises from nearly every page of the New Testament. Statistically speaking, the two emotions most frequently expressed and encouraged are joy and thanksgiving. This emotional fullness comes out clearly in the many "hymns" recorded by the canonical authors. Members of churches employing the ancient liturgies will be familiar with those songs of praise found in the early chapters of Luke's Gospel: the Magnificat of Mary ("My soul magnifies the Lord, and my spirit rejoices in God my Savior . . . ," Luke 1:46–55); the Benedictus, reported by Luke to have been spoken by Zechariah under the influence of the Holy Spirit ("Blessed be the Lord God of Israel, for he has visited and redeemed his people . . . ," Luke 1:68–79); and the Nunc Dimittis, prayed by old Simeon as he cradled the infant Jesus in his arms ("Lord, now lettest thou thy servant depart in peace, according to thy word; for mine eyes have seen thy salvation . . . ," Luke 2:29–35). We may guess that Luke placed these celebrative verses in his Gospel either because he found them already used, then as now, in the church's worship, or because he wished them to become models for that worship.[2]

Another hymn known to nearly all contemporary Christians is the magnificent Prologue to the Fourth Gospel: "In the beginning was the Word, and the Word was with God, and the Word was God . . ." (John 1:1). This dramatic ode on the incarnation climaxes in the famous fourteenth verse: "And the Word became flesh and dwelt among us, full of grace and truth." Less familiar, perhaps, are the hymns recorded in Phil. 2:5ff. ("Have this mind among yourselves, which you have in Christ Jesus, who, though he was in the form of God, did not count equality with God a thing to be grasped, but emptied himself, taking the form of a servant . . ."); in Col. 1:15ff. ("He is the image of the invisible God, the first-born of all creation . . ."; see also I Cor. 8:6); and in I Tim. 3:16 ("He was manifested in the flesh, vindicated in the Spirit, seen by angels, preached among the nations, believed on in the world, taken up in glory"). The book of Revelation too abounds with songs of blessing sung by saints and angels in heaven (see, for example, Rev. 4:11; 5:9f.; 11:17ff.; 15:3ff.; 19:1ff.). At one point in Romans, Paul breaks into a spontaneous, almost ecstatic, hymn of praise to God:

> O the depth of the riches and wisdom and knowledge of God! How unsearchable are his judgments and how inscrutable his ways!
>> "For who has known the mind of the Lord,
>> or who has been his counselor?"
>> "Or who has given a gift to him
>> that he might be repaid?"
> For from him and through him and to him are all things. To him be glory for ever. Amen. (Rom. 11:33–36)

No doubt there were many more hymns which, though current in the early church, failed to find their way into the New Testament. In Ephesians it is suggested that early Christian worship was a time of great musical creativity. Thus the author of the epistle urges believers to address one another

> in psalms and hymns and spiritual songs, singing and making melody to the Lord with all your heart, always and for everything giving thanks in the name of our Lord Jesus Christ to God the Father. (Eph. 5:19f.)

How different, even in conception, from most Christian worship today! Customarily, we sing songs from a book to the backs of other people's heads. The result is that our "praises" often sound somewhat less inspiring than funeral dirges. Not so with the New Testament hymns. In every passage cited above, the emotional notes struck most frequently are joy and thanksgiving.

Literary evidence for the predominance of gratitude in the emotional lives of early Christians may also be found in the so-called thanksgiving formulas that introduce Paul's letters. To the Corinthians, Paul writes:

> I give thanks to God always for you because of the grace of God which was given you in Christ Jesus, that in every way you were enriched in him with all speech and all knowledge . . . so that you are not lacking in any spiritual gift *(charisma),* as you wait for the revealing of our Lord Jesus Christ. (I Cor. 1:4–7)

Here Paul gives thanks specifically for the abundance of charismata which God has lavished upon the congregation. Similar formulas occur in Rom. 1:8ff.; Phil. 1:3ff.; I Thess. 1:2ff.; II Thess. 1: 3; Philemon 4; Col. 1:3ff.; Eph. 1:15ff. In many of these Paul (or a Pauline disciple) thanks God for the faith and love manifested by the believers he is addressing, that is, for the use they have made of their gifts. Thanksgiving formulas as such are relatively common in the secular letters of the first century. Paul did not invent the literary structure. Nevertheless, in his important work, *Form and Function of the Pauline Thanksgivings,* Paul Schubert concludes that "Paul uses these terms [for thanksgiving] more frequently, in a greater variety of functions and with stronger emphasis than any other comparable unit of sources."[3] For Paul, thanksgiving throbbed at the heart of Christian existence. How could it be otherwise for a people so richly blessed?

The very word for sharing the Christian faith verbally reflects feelings of rejoicing and thanksgiving. The Greek verb *euangelizomai* literally means "to proclaim the gospel," especially to those who have never heard it. The substance of this gospel is, of course, God's act for the world's redemption in the ministry, death, and resurrection of Jesus. What interests us here is not so much the content of the message as the fact that the telling of the gospel itself expresses a sense of giftedness on the part of the early Christians. "Good news!" they shouted to all who would listen. "We have been blessed beyond imagination by God. Here is how it happened. It can happen to you too. Believe our message so that you can take part in our joy and praise" (a free paraphrase of Acts, ch. 2; see also Rom. 15:7–13). There was an urgency, a spontaneity, even a compulsion about the preaching of the Christian message which distinguished it at the very outset from the propaganda of most other religious movements in the first century. Christians seem to have felt themselves so filled to overflowing with the gifts of God that they *had* to share their good fortune. Thus, when the early church in Jerusalem found itself forbidden by local authorities to preach in Jesus' name, Peter replied: "We cannot but speak of what we have seen and heard" (Acts 4:20). Similarly, Paul wrote of the "necessity" laid upon him to preach the gospel (I Cor. 9:16). It was as if these early Christians felt they would be committing a grievous sin by not speaking; they would be depriving others of joy.

The proclamation of the good news also became an occasion for thanksgiving. Above all, it produced gratitude in those who witnessed its progress. Paul tells the Corinthians that his ministry of preaching "is all for your sake, so that as grace extends to more and more people it may increase thanksgiving, to the glory of God" (II Cor. 4:15). Where the gifts of God were shared, emotions of fullness abounded in preacher, new believers, and believing witnesses alike. This happened not least because according to the New Testament writers miraculous events regularly accompanied the proclamation of the good news (Acts 3:1–7; 4:29ff.; 8:4–7; I Cor. 2:1–5; II Cor. 12:11f.; Gal. 3:1–5).

While joy and thanksgiving seem to stand in the foreground when New Testament authors describe the giftedness they and their readers experience, other positive emotions emerge as well. Hope is often mentioned (Acts 28:20; Rom. 5:2–5; 8:20–25; 15:13; Gal. 5:5; Heb. 6:11, 18; 7:19; I Peter 1:3, 21; 3:15; I John 3:3), for it is hope, given with faith, that allows believers to conceptualize the great future they will inherit. Also associated with the giftedness of the gospel is a sense of tranquillity. This is not the Stoic philosopher's ideal of impassability, a state of no emotion at all, but the Old Testament *shalom,* which inspires feelings of well-being and wholeness. The New Testament translates *shalom* with the word "peace." To the readers of the Fourth Gospel, Jesus says: "Peace I leave with you; my peace I give to you; not as the world gives do I give to you. Let not your hearts be troubled, neither let them be afraid" (John 14:27). Paul calls this peace a fruit of the Spirit (Gal. 5:22) or "the peace of God which passes all understanding" (Phil. 4:7).

A third prominent emotion that serves to reveal the giftedness felt by New Testament believers we might call the confidence of faith. It is the conviction that God stands near to help the believer prevail over great obstacles. Paul expresses this beautifully in the triumphant words that close the eighth chapter of Romans:

> I am sure that neither death, nor life, nor angels, nor principalities, nor things present, nor things to come, nor powers, nor height, nor depth, nor anything else in all creation, will be able to separate us from the love of God in Christ Jesus our Lord. (Rom. 8:38f.)

Here we see the reflective side of faith which assures believers that the God who has called them will remain faithful to the work he has begun in them (Phil. 1:6; 2:13; I Thess. 5:23f.). But faith also possesses an extroverted quality that shows itself in feelings of boldness as one preaches the gospel or deals pastorally with sister and brother believers. In Acts, members of the Jerusalem church pray for and receive the power to speak God's word "with all boldness" (Acts 4:13, 29, 31; 28:31). Paul describes his ministry as one of boldness (II Cor. 3:12; 7:4) and proves it by pressuring the believer Philemon to welcome his runaway slave Onesimus back again as a "brother" (Philemon 8–16). There is probably no limit to the emotional breadth of abundant life. But for now we can content ourselves with noticing which kinds of feelings surface most often in the New Testament writings.

The Language of Giftedness

Let us take a closer look at some of the words and phrases most frequently used to express these emotions so that we can learn something about the life situations that produced them. Even the language about gifts in the New Testament confronts us with an embarrassment of riches. Quite apart from the words for "joy" *(chara)*, "rejoicing" *(chairō)*, and "thanksgiving" *(eucharistia or eucharisteō)*, we find no fewer than seven different Greek nouns that can be translated "gift" *(doma, dosis, dōrea, dōrēma, dōron, charis, charisma)*. Each of these may refer to something God graciously bestows upon humankind. In addition, the Greek words for "blessing," "abundance," "riches," "distribution," and "measure" are often used to describe divine gifts.

We encounter a similar phenomenon when we come to the verbs that denote the act of giving. The basic verb, *didōmi*, occurs well over a hundred times with God, Jesus, or the Holy Spirit as the subject who grants blessings to humans. Three variants of *didōmi*, as well as five other Greek verbs, may also describe the transmission of divine gifts. This very proliferation of words for "gift" and "giving" serves to confirm our initial impression that the New Testament writers felt themselves and their readers to be extraordinarily blessed.[4]

It would not be profitable for us to examine the nuances of every one of these words. We are more interested in the experiences within the early church which gave rise to their use. Nevertheless, we must devote special attention to the word group that centers around the stem *char* (pronounced *kyar*), for it is from this stem that the profound name for "grace" *(charis)* and the virtually unique New Testament word for "gift" *(charisma)* develop. Significantly, the nouns for "joy" *(chara)* and "thanks" *(eucharistia)*, evolve from the same stem. It is with these words, already familiar to us as the predominant emotions expressed in the New Testament, that we shall ask our experiential questions. What kinds of situations occasioned rejoicing among New Testament Christians? For what, precisely, did they give thanks?

The early believers found great joy in the simple fact that they believed. Without any merit on their part they had been allowed to discover the Kingdom of God—like the man who stumbles across a treasure hidden in a field and "then in his joy . . . goes and sells all that he has and buys that field" (Matt. 13:44). When Paul and Silas proclaimed salvation to the terrified jailer of Philippi, he responded in faith and celebrated a midnight banquet with his former prisoners, where "he rejoiced with all his household that he had believed in God" (Acts 16:34; see also I Peter 1:8). God's angels are said to rejoice over the repentance of a single sinner (Luke 15:10). Probably the Gospel writer intends that this response should apply also to the church. In its mutual forgiveness it too will resemble the shepherd who loses a sheep, the woman who loses a coin, and the father who loses his prodigal son, but then receives each one back with great rejoicing (Luke 15:3–24). Fellowship with Jesus, especially after the resurrection, produced great joy among his followers. Jesus anticipates this glow of reunion in John 16:22: "So you have sorrow now, but I will see you again, and your hearts will rejoice, and no one will take your joy from you." According to the fourth Evangelist, Jesus' prophecy found its initial fulfillment on the evening of the resurrection when he "came and stood among [his disciples] and said to them, 'Peace be with you.' When he had said this, he showed them his hands and his side. Then the disciples were glad when they saw the Lord" (John 20:19f.; see also Luke 24:41). The joyous communal meals of the early church (Acts 2:46) seem to have been understood as a continuation of this fellowship with the risen Christ. Similarly, the jubilant participation in the power of Jesus' name which had begun with his disciples' ministry of exorcism (Luke 10:17) reappeared among the earliest Jerusalem believers in the form of healing miracles (Acts 3:6–8; 4: 29f.; 5:15–16).

Corresponding to the gladness that surrounded fellowship with Christ is that which characterized the close relationships among brother and sister believers. Paul calls the Philippians "my joy and my crown" (Phil. 4:1). To the Corinthians he writes, "I rejoice at the coming of Stephanas and Fortunatus and Achaicus, because they have made up for your absence; for they refreshed my spirit as well as yours" (I Cor. 16:17f.; see also Rom. 15:32). The author of II John longs to see his readers face-to-face "so that our joy may be complete" (II John 12). For Paul, the fact that Jews and Gentiles can praise the God of Israel together in the church is cause for rejoicing (Rom. 15:7–13). New Testament writers also derive great joy from the transformed behavior of their readers. Thus Paul expresses his satisfaction with the faith and love demonstrated by the Thessalonians (I Thess. 2:18ff.; 3:6–9; see also Rom. 16:19). In III John the elder tells his addressee Gaius:

> I greatly rejoiced when some of the brethren arrived and testified to the truth of your life, as indeed you do follow the truth. No greater joy can I have than this, to hear that my children follow the truth. (III John 3f.)

New Testament believers can even find joy in their trials (Heb. 10:34). The author of I Peter 4:13 urges his readers to rejoice "in so far as you share Christ's sufferings, that you may also rejoice and be glad when his glory is revealed." This counsel, which may strike us as almost masochistic, will receive closer attention in Chapter 5.

Since the Greek words for rejoicing and thanksgiving derive from the same stem *(char)*, it is not surprising that occasions for rejoicing in the New Testament sometimes coincide exactly with occasions for thanksgiving. Thus, just as believers rejoice "in the Lord," so they respond to God with thanksgiving "through Christ" for the Lord's peace, for his rich words of wisdom, and for the power to act which he grants (Col. 3:15–17). Similarly, the nourishing fellowship with one's cobelievers becomes an object for thanksgiving as well as rejoicing. Paul writes to the Philippians:

> I thank my God for all my remembrance of you, always in every prayer of mine for you all making my prayer with joy, thankful for your partnership *(koinōnia)* in the gospel from the first day until now. (Phil. 1:3ff.)

Luke reports that when Paul, under Roman guard, is met on the outskirts of Rome by some believers who have journeyed from the city to welcome him, he experiences them as a refreshing gift. "On seeing them Paul thanked God and took courage." (Acts 28:15.) As with rejoicing, the behavior of other Christians provides cause for thanksgiving. Paul most often expresses gratitude for the faith and/or love of his readers (Rom. 1:8; I Thess. 1:2; II Thess. 1:3; Philemon 4). But on one occasion he also thanks God for the Thessalonians' eager response to the gospel (I Thess. 2:13); and once he promises the Corinthians that their generous giving will

> produce thanksgiving to God; for the rendering of this service not only supplies the wants of the saints but also overflows in many thanksgivings to God. (II Cor. 9:11f.)

Finally, just as the expansion of the gospel results in rejoicing among Christians (Acts 11:23; 15:3; Phil. 1:18), so it also increases thanksgiving "to the glory of God" (II Cor. 4:15).

As we might expect, New Testament believers, like those in the Old Testament, thanked God for their meals (Acts 27:35), and indeed for all of creation; "for everything created by God is good, and nothing is to be rejected if it is received with thanksgiving, for then it is consecrated [literally, "sanctified"] by the word of God and prayer" (I Tim. 4:4). We should note in passing that nothing in the New Testament resembles Psalm 104, the lengthy, beautifully detailed hymn of praise offered to God for the glories of creation. Yet the New Testament would hardly oppose such thanksgiving. In fact, psalms like this probably found their way into early Christian worship (see Col. 3:16; Eph. 5:19). As we suggested in the previous chapter, we must here use the Old Testament to complete our picture of the "stuff" of New Testament giftedness. Acknowledging this steady influence of the Old Testament upon the New saves us from jumping to a conclusion, as too many careless Christians have done, namely, that believers ought to find their joy chiefly in otherworldly gifts. In fact, our study of the *char* stem words leads in just the opposite direction. The gifts most often mentioned in connection with rejoicing and thanksgiving are horizontal, interpersonal gifts which can be enjoyed in this world.

Grace and Gifts

Yet we must hasten to add that these gifts ought not to be described as "natural," if we mean by "natural" that which happens as a matter of course to most people most of the time. The evidence suggests that New Testament Christians found themselves capable of seeing gifts everywhere, of considering as gifts people and situations that others found, at most, pleasant. If they could rejoice and thank God more than their contemporaries, that was because they possessed an unusual consciousness of God's gracious activity in their lives. Much that seemed ordinary had become extraordinary in their eyes because they now perceived and named it as a blessing pouring forth from the God and Father of Jesus Christ. The word that the New Testament uses most frequently to describe God's magnanimity toward undeserving humans is *charis,* "grace." The awareness of grace transforms what believers receive into gifts *from God,* whether they be "natural" or "supernatural" according to the philosophical and scientific standards of the day. Grace is understood in the New Testament above all as a favorable inclination on God's part. It is his reaching out in love toward humankind, most clearly in the words and events surrounding Jesus' ministry (John 1:14–16; Acts 20:32; Rom. 3:24; 5:1f.; I Cor. 15:10; II Cor. 8:9; Eph. 2:8f.; Heb. 2:9; I Peter 5:10). Through faith, men and women "receive" this goodness of God (Rom. 1:5; Eph. 2:8). Grace finds a home with us so that Christ lives in us (Rom. 8:9ff.) and we in him (I Cor. 12:12f.). Then a sense of fullness results and everything can be seen as a potential gift. "He who did not spare his own Son but gave him up for us all, will he not also give us all things with him?" (Rom. 8:32.) The logic seems to be that if God has offered up Jesus, a part of himself, then he will surely grant to believers all lesser things in such a way that they too become mediators of grace, i.e., gifts.

Grace is not an emotion. Nor can the faith that receives it be described simply as emotion. Faith clearly has an intellectual side to it; one must know something *about* whatever one believes in. Yet when grace comes, emotions inevitably stir, particularly the emotions of joy and thanksgiving. Paul conceives of grace and thanksgiving as two parts of a cycle. Grace *(charis)* comes from God, takes hold in humans, and returns to God by way of thanksgiving *(eucharistia)*. Thus the apostle can write that "as grace extends to more and more people [through the preaching of the gospel] it [will] increase thanksgiving to the glory of God" (II Cor. 4:15). A few chapters later, Paul urges the reluctant Corinthians to complete a collection of money (which he sometimes calls a *charis!*) for poor believers in Jerusalem. Paul argues that they, the Corinthians, will accomplish even more with their contribution than the financial relief of the impoverished saints. They will also produce thanksgiving to God *(eucharistia)* when the Jerusalemites praise him for the grace *(charis)* he has placed into the Corinthians to fulfill this task (II Cor. 9:11–14). And who among the Corinthians (Paul implies) would want to deny that God had given them grace? Indeed, who would want to deny God his rightful share of thanksgiving? To crown his playful argument, Paul concludes with a double entendre thanksgiving of his own: "Thanks *(charis)* be to God for his inexpressible gift *(dōrea)!*" (II Cor. 9:15). After laboring to explain the whole process of grace, Paul can only throw up his hands and confess that it is, after all, inexpressible. All he can finally say is that God receives his "grace" by bestowing it. Intertwined with the horizontal giving of believers to one another is a constant vertical stream of *charis* from God and *eucharistia* to God.

So grace produces the emotional responses of joy and thanksgiving (as well as others). Yet not even joy and thanksgiving are emotional responses pure and simple. They also contain an element of will. This shows in the fact that Paul and the other New Testament writers can issue *commands* to rejoice and give thanks:

Rejoice in the Lord always; again I will say, Rejoice! (Phil. 4:4)

Rejoice with those who rejoice, weep with those who weep. (Rom. 12:15)

Count it all joy, my brethren, when you meet various trials, for you know that the testing of your faith produces steadfastness. (James 1:2f.)

And let the peace of Christ rule in your hearts, to which indeed you were called in the one body. And be thankful. (Col. 3:15)

Rejoice always, pray constantly, give thanks in all circumstances; for this is the will of God in Christ Jesus for you. (I Thess. 5:16f.)

For everything created by God is good, and nothing is to be rejected if it is received with thanksgiving; for then it is consecrated by the word of God and prayer. (I Tim. 4:4f.)

It is not altogether "natural," even for those who have received grace, to thank and rejoice. All humans, including believers, grow sluggish about recognizing and receiving gifts. We forget the gifts surrounding us, so we need to be reminded of their omnipresence. That is one obvious reason for the commands. Some of the passages above, however, give us the impression that there must be more to this required thanking and rejoicing than a memory jog. In Rom. 12:15, for example, rejoicing appears to be an act of love, done for the sake of the other person. According to I Thess. 5:16f., the reason given for rejoicing and thanking is that it fulfills God's will. In I Tim. 4:4f. thanksgiving looks less like an emotion than a work of sanctification performed upon God's creation.[5] The act of thanking is even called "the word of God and prayer." Perhaps the author has in mind Biblical words used in a thanksgiving prayer. At any rate, he wishes to say that thanksgiving cannot be just a human response; it is, initially, a divine prescription, a word of God. Ultimately, it means that humans must give God the praise he deserves by naming a gift as his. Thanksgiving abounds to his glory (II Cor. 4:15). It is his grace coming back to him (II Cor. 9: 15), all the richer in his eyes for its having been received and put to use. A passage from Isaiah expresses the thought well: "So shall my word be that goes forth from my mouth; it shall not return to me empty, but it shall accomplish that which I purpose, and prosper in the thing for which I sent it" (Isa. 55:11).

The notion that New Testament thanksgiving can be understood as something more than a feeling of gratitude helps to illumine two passages that might otherwise remain obscure. Commenting upon the worship services held in Corinth, Paul writes:

> If you bless with the Spirit [i.e., by praying in unintelligible tongues], how can any one in the position of an outsider say the "Amen" to your thanksgiving when he does not know what you are saying? For you may give thanks well enough, but the other man is not edified. (I Cor. 14:16f.)

Paul's words show that he thinks of thanksgiving in worship not as a private emotional affair between the individual and God but as a means of building up the neighbor. The "outsider" may be a catechumen, a chance visitor, or perhaps someone not blessed with the gift of interpreting tongues. Thanksgiving spoken in plain language will help the neighbor also to acknowledge God's gifts, thus multiplying thanksgiving to God. In the corporate body of believers it is not enough for a worshiper to build himself up by thanking God in tongues. Here thanksgiving must become an intelligible, willed act of worship that heightens the whole church's sense of giftedness. Through the rational effort of one believer to spell out in words what he or she feels thankful for, all become enriched.

The second passage is Luke's narration of Paul's voyage as a prisoner from Crete to Malta on the way to Rome. When the apostle's ship gets caught in a violent storm, everyone aboard despairs of surviving. Although food is available, no one feels like eating. Just then Paul comes forward with the claim that an angel has appeared to him and said: "Do not be afraid, Paul; you must stand before Caesar; and lo, God has granted you all those who sail with you" (Acts 27:24). Here we catch sight of a graceful irony typical of the New Testament. According to the angel, Paul's captors have been delivered, for their safety, into the hands of their prisoner. The apostle declares his faith in the angel's message and urges his shipmates to take heart, since (so he believes) they will surely be saved. It is not until the next day, however, that they begin to take his words seriously. For then, in a remarkable scene at dawn, Paul exhorts them to break their long fast and strengthen themselves, promising that "not a hair is to perish from the head of any of you" (Acts 27:34). The text continues:

> And when he had said this, he took bread, and giving thanks to God *(eucharistēsen)* in the presence of all he broke it and began to eat. Then they all were encouraged and ate some food themselves. (Acts 27:35f.)

In the midst of a storm and a crowd of frightened pagans Paul celebrates a "eucharist." We cannot be sure whether Luke intended this meal to be understood as a Lord's Supper, but the thought must have occurred to his earliest readers. In any event, this thanksgiving meal, like Jesus' supper with his disciples in the upper room, transforms the situation. Despondent seasick men come alive. Paul's eucharistic act, done in faith, blesses the entire company, despite the fact that they are not believers. Such is the power inherent in the naming of God's gifts before him. A well-known painting by Norman Rockwell depicts an old woman praying over her meal in a busy lunchroom. Seated beside her is a small boy who might be her grandson. Looking on, partly offended and partly convicted by the woman's reverence, are some factory workers and office clerks, all male. One can see toughness in their faces, but a certain awe is there as well. In a small though powerful way the woman's public thanksgiving to God has momentarily turned their lives around.

We have been saying that it was grace which enabled the early Christians to perceive large numbers of people, events, and material goods as gifts. But for some readers grace may seem to be nothing more than an abstract idea, elusive as a puff of smoke. Indeed, it *is* virtually impossible to do justice to the grandeur of grace with words. Still, for the New Testament believers grace was anything but ethereal. They experienced it as altogether solid and concrete, for it had given them new lives. This substantiality reveals itself in the tendency of the word *charis* to describe particular facets of God's good favor incarnate in specific situations. We have already noticed that the word can mean "thanks," as in the phrase

"Thanks be to God" (Rom. 6:17; 7:25; I Cor. 15:57; II Cor. 8:16; 9:15). The Septuagint version of the Old Testament sometimes uses *charis* for the good favor of God which makes one person physically or emotionally attractive to another. This nuance appears in Acts 2:47. When Luke writes that the earliest believers in Jerusalem had "favor with all the people," he means that the Jews of Jerusalem found them good and acceptable. Several times Paul associates the collection he is raising for believers in Jerusalem with the word *charis.* Once he calls the money itself a *charis* (I Cor. 16: 3). A good translation would be "thank offering." Elsewhere the word denotes the process of collection (II Cor. 8:6–7, 19) or the motivation for giving (II Cor. 8:1; 9:8, 14). Here, *charis,* though specific to the occasion, manifests itself in several forms. It is simultaneously material object, process, and power. It is located in a given spot, but it can never be enclosed in a single definition. Like the God who sends it, it remains free. Paul also uses *charis* to refer to the gift and task of his apostolic work among the Gentiles, or the strength to fulfill this calling (Rom. 1:5; 15:1f.; I Cor. 5:8–11; Gal. 2:9). In these passages too the word has to do with something concrete yet mysteriously broad. Paul speaks of his *charis* as a gift tailored precisely to him. Yet it is not a gift that can be separated from his person and placed under the control of his will, for in some sense it also constitutes his whole apostolic identity. "By the grace of God I am what I am." (I Cor. 15:10.) Finally, there are at least four passages that link *charis* with the special gifts thought by the canonical authors to be revealing themselves in every New Testament church:

Having gifts *(charismata)* that differ according to the grace *(charis)* given to us, let us use them: if prophecy, in proportion to our faith; if service, in our serving; he who teaches, in his teaching. (Rom. 12: 6f.)

I give thanks to God always for you because of the grace *(charis)* of God which was given you in Christ Jesus, that in every way you were enriched in him with all speech and all knowledge . . . so that you are not lacking in any spiritual gift *(charisma),* as you wait for the revealing of our Lord Jesus Christ. (I Cor. 1:4–7)

But grace *(charis)* was given to each of us according to the measure of Christ's gift *(dōrea).* Therefore it is said,
> "When he ascended on high he led
> a host of captives,
> and he gave gifts to men."

... And his gifts *(didōmi)* were that some should be apostles, some prophets, some evangelists, some pastors and teachers, . . . for the work of ministry, for building up the body of Christ. (Eph. 4:7–8, 11–12)

As each has received a gift *(charisma),* employ it for one another, as good stewards of God's varied grace *(charis).* (I Peter 4:10)

We shall have more to say about these passages, and particularly about the word *charisma,* in Chapter 4. Here we simply want to note that like the other *charis* passages we have been examining, they display the tendency for grace to manifest itself in ways that are concrete and differentiated. Grace shapes itself to individuals and situations so that through them God can work out his purposes. In this sense every gift of grace is unique, precisely suited to the person or occasion.

Giftedness: An Expanding Category

Let us now examine some phenomena which the early Christians called gifts but which the average person, both in the first century and in our own time, would not readily identify as such. This exercise will reinforce our impression that New Testament believers felt extraordinarily blessed and therefore saw God's gracious hand where others did not. We have already mentioned the story of Paul's voyage as a prisoner. The angel's message that God had granted to Paul all who sailed with him would not have struck Jewish readers as odd, for similar phrases occur in the Old Testament (Josh. 8:1; Judg. 7:2; I Sam. 17:46). But there the sense is that those given over by God to another will be punished or destroyed by the recipient. In Acts we have just the opposite: the ship's crew and passengers, including Paul's captors, are given to him so that they can share in his blessing. Those given over receive the gift of their lives.

Mark 13:11 describes a situation in which believers are put on trial before synagogue councils and Gentile officials alike. Jesus promises that in those days they will not be without divine help:

> And when they bring you to trial and deliver you up, do not be anxious beforehand what you are to say; but say whatever is given to you in that hour, for it is not you who speak, but the Holy Spirit. (Mark 13:11)

Here the gift to be granted consists of a faithful confession. Again, Jews would be reminded of Old Testament figures such as Moses and the prophets who became God's mouthpieces through the operation of the Spirit. But the claim that *all* believers will share in this privilege when called upon to give an account of themselves is quite unique. Such defenses were not, and still are not, usually called gifts.

Another uncommon gift, this time one not given to all believers, is described in Matt. 19:10ff. Here the disciples react with dismay to Jesus' strict teaching regarding the permanence of the marriage vow. "If such is the case of a man with his wife," they say, "it is not expedient to marry." Jesus replies:

> Not all men can receive this saying [i.e., "it is not expedient to marry"], but only those to whom it is given. For there are eunuchs who have been so from birth, and there are eunuchs who have been made eunuchs by men, and there are eunuchs who have made themselves eunuchs for the sake of the kingdom of heaven. He who is able to receive this, let him receive it. (Matt. 19:11f.)

According to Matthew's report, Jesus teaches that life without marriage requires a special "gift." In the first two cases we might be more inclined to talk about "necessity." Paul echoes this teaching when he calls his own celibate state a *charisma* (I Cor. 7:7).

Surprisingly, the New Testament sometimes places the good works done by Christians in the category of gift. According to Eph. 2:10, God has prepared good works from all eternity for believers to "walk in." Moreover, he provides them with "every blessing in abundance, so that [they] may always have enough of everything and may provide in abundance for every good work" (II Cor. 9: 8). God's magnanimity does not, of course, remove the weight of responsibility from believers. They can refuse to perform their preordained works. Yet the Biblical manner of speaking encourages us to think of even our best productions as if they were ultimately initiated by God. "I worked harder than any of them," wrote Paul, "though it was not I, but the grace of God which is with me" (I Cor. 15:10).

Several passages in the New Testament witness to the giftlike quality of suffering. We shall treat some of these texts in more detail later, but it is useful to introduce them here:

> Shall I not drink the cup which the Father has given me? (Jesus to Peter in John 18:11)

> We rejoice in our sufferings, knowing that suffering produces endurance, and endurance produces character, and character produces hope. (Rom. 5:3f.)

> Blessed be the God and Father of our Lord Jesus Christ, the Father of all mercies and God of all comfort, who comforts us in all our affliction. . . . For as we share abundantly in Christ's sufferings, so through Christ we share abundantly in comfort too. (II Cor. 1:3–5)

> For it has been granted to you that for the sake of Christ you should not only believe in him but also suffer for his sake. (Phil. 1:29)

> But rejoice in so far as you share Christ's sufferings, that you may also rejoice and be glad when his glory is revealed. (I Peter 4:13)

A curious passage, which probably fits in this category as well, is II Cor. 12:7. There Paul reports that after his visionary journey to the third heaven "a thorn was given me in the flesh, a messenger of Satan, to harass me, to keep me from being too elated." Although he labels the thorn a messenger of Satan, Paul the Jew would naturally have conceived of Satan as operating only by God's consent (see Job 6:6ff.). Hence when he calls the thorn "given," he means that even this physical torment comes in some sense from God. It is God's purpose, not Satan's, to keep him from becoming too proud.

As a final example of how early Christians expanded the definition of gift, let us examine Rom. 15:29. Here Paul tells his readers that after delivering the collection from his Gentile churches to the Jewish believers in Jerusalem, he will come immediately to them "in the fulness of the blessing of Christ." Probably this fullness should be identified with a flood of thanksgiving to God from the Jerusalem Christians which Paul hopes to witness when he delivers the gift (II Cor. 9:12ff.; Rom. 15:25–32). Few of us would think of calling such an event "the fulness of the blessing of Christ." Such language seems overinflated. But Paul, who believes that his whole ministry is pressing toward the unification of Israel with Gentile believers (Rom. 11:13ff., 25ff.; 15:19ff.), stands convinced that God's favor toward him prior to Jesus' return from heaven will climax in precisely this historical moment. We note in passing that the great blessing Paul expects is not what we would ordinarily call mystical or otherworldly. It seems most akin to the satisfaction we would feel upon being told by a superior that we had completed an assigned task with high distinction. "Well done, good and faithful servant; . . . enter into the joy of your master." (Matt. 25:21.)

A Warning Against Shallow Celebration

Thus far we have been emphasizing the consciousness on the part of New Testament believers that they were receiving extraordinary blessings. This resulted, we said, in a sense of great fullness, which in turn spilled out in the emotions most frequently expressed by the New Testament writers: joy and thanksgiving. It was consistent with the intention of the texts, we noted, to view the New Testament as a continuous celebration of God's new blessings in Jesus Christ.

But now we must qualify those statements in order to present a more accurate picture of the New Testament witness. Giftedness? Fullness? Celebration? Yes, but not if these three degenerate into a form of "heavenly" existence which is constantly blinding itself to the dangers and sufferings of "this world." Not if the giftedness, fullness, and celebration function as excuses for ignoring common decency or developing one's own spiritual gifts at the expense of the neighbor's welfare. At one stage of its history the Corinthian congregation seems to have fallen into this shallow sort of celebration. In the letter that we know as I Corinthians, Paul responded to the situation with great force.

The apostle begins by giving thanks for the Corinthian congregation, since, as he notes, they are "not lacking in any spiritual gift" (*charisma;* I Cor. 1:7). But despite their authentic giftedness, they cannot be addressed as "spiritual men" (*pneumatikoi;* I Cor. 3:1ff.). Instead, he says, he must call them "babes in Christ." The jealousy and strife evident in the congregation's factionalism make it clear to Paul that they have not used their spiritual gifts as God intended them to be used, namely, to build up their neighbors. As far as their behavior is concerned, the Corinthians differ little from unbelievers (I Cor. 3:3; 6:1–8). They have allowed their sense of giftedness to *replace* their sense of responsibility.

The heart of their problem is a form of intoxication. Their frivolous enjoyment of the new life in Christ has become, like the misuse of drugs and alcohol, an escape from the harsh realities of the material world. In one of his most sarcastic outbursts Paul accuses the Corinthians of practicing cheap spirituality:

> Already you are filled! Already you have become rich! Without us you have become kings! And would that you did reign, so that we might share the rule with you! For I think that God has exhibited us apostles as last of all, like men sentenced to death; because we have become a spectacle to the world, to angels and to men. We are fools for Christ's sake, but you are wise in Christ. We are weak, but you are strong. You are held in honor, but we in disrepute. (I Cor. 4:8–11)

Paul claims that the apostles know something that the Corinthians do not know (or have forgotten): true celebration of life with Christ takes place in the midst of foolishness, weakness, disrepute, and death. It never just cancels them out. The Corinthians resemble the young woman mentioned at the beginning of this chapter who was edging toward a nervous breakdown. Like her, they do not want to acknowledge the dark side of life. Their joy and thanksgiving amount to little more than giddiness. Hence, their celebration produces a morality that condones incest in the congregation (I Cor. 5:1ff.), permits believers to sue one another in civil courts (I Cor. 6:1ff.), combines Christian piety with pagan religious practices—which probably include intercourse with temple prostitutes (I Cor. 10:14–22; 6:12–20)—leads to drunkenness at the Lord's Supper (I Cor. 11:20ff.), and results in chaotic worship services where each person exercises his or her spiritual gift without regard to the edification of other believers and visitors (I Cor. 14:20–39).

It is in I Corinthians that Paul warns his readers to consider the example of Israel: though the first generation of God's chosen people was blessed with extraordinary spiritual food (manna) and drink (water from the rock at Horeb), most of them fell away from God through the practice of immorality and perished (I Cor. 10: 1–10). To the filled and gifted Corinthians, Paul writes: "Let any one who thinks that he stands take heed lest he fall" (I Cor. 10: 12). Upon these worshipers, who bask in the glory in their communion with the risen Christ, the apostle lays a sober teaching regarding the Lord's Supper:

> As often as you eat this bread and drink the cup, you proclaim the Lord's death until he comes.
>
> Whoever, therefore, eats the bread or drinks the cup of the Lord in an unworthy manner will be guilty of profaning the body and blood of the Lord. Let a man examine himself, and so eat of the bread and drink of the cup. For any one who eats and drinks without discerning the body eats and drinks judgment upon himself. That is why many of you are weak and ill, and some have died.
>
> (I Cor. 11:26–30)

Contrary to appearances, Paul is not trying to squelch celebration. He favors joy and thanksgiving quite as much as any other New Testament writer. If Paul were writing to an average Protestant or Roman Catholic congregation in the United States today, he would almost certainly encourage *more* visible enjoyment of God's gifts in Christ. In I Corinthians, however, the apostle's purpose is to ground his flighty readers by acquainting them with the depth of true celebration. Real giftedness displays itself in humility (Rom. 12:3ff.), in a sense of need for God's daily renewal (Matt. 6:11; II Cor. 4:16), in the awareness of how much evil must yet be overcome (I Cor. 15:22ff.; Rom. 7:13–25), and in the earthy task of loving one's neighbor (I Cor. 12:31 to 14:19). Real celebration does not deny suffering or death, as the Corinthians appear to have done (I Cor. 11:30; 15:12ff.); it encompasses them (I Cor. 15: 31; II Cor. 12:9f.). More on this theme in Chapter 5. Here it is enough to recognize that the core experience of the New Testament church, giftedness, proves to be as kaleidoscopic as it is widespread. We can hardly study it without standing in awe of it.

CHAPTER 3

Holy Spirit: The Nearness of the Giver

The New Testament church felt itself repeatedly enriched by the many-splendored gifts of God. Because of this ongoing experience the first believers concluded that they were living in an absolutely unique era of human history. Never before, they imagined, had God rained such abundant blessings down upon the earth. Indeed, this richness must mean that the end of Israel's protracted trials was now at hand.

Jesus himself had proclaimed that the long-awaited Kingdom of God was dawning in his ministry (Matt. 12:28; Luke 11:20). According to Acts, Peter interpreted the arrival of the Spirit at Pentecost as a fulfillment of God's Old Testament promises to Israel ("And in the last days it shall be, God declares, that I will pour out my Spirit on all flesh"; Acts 2:17, from Joel 2:28). Paul referred to the events surrounding Jesus' ministry as "the fulness of . . . time" (Gal. 4:4). For him, the world situation after the resurrection was one of "new creation" (II Cor. 5:17; Gal. 6:15). In fact, he concluded that the period in which he lived had to be nothing less than the reign of Christ (I Cor. 15:24f.).

With even greater boldness the author of the Fourth Gospel sketched a Jesus who proclaimed his advent as a timeless Now in which believers could enjoy eternal life even prior to death (John 5:24). Already during his ministry, he said, the judgment of "this world" and the downfall of Satan were taking place (John 12:31f.). All the New Testament writers of course regarded God in Christ as the Ultimate Cause of this unique salvific time. But the sign of its presence most frequently named by them was the Holy Spirit.

God's Spirit as Mediator of the New Abundance

The descent of the Dove marked Jesus' baptism as a messianic anointing (Matt. 3:13–17; Mark 1:9–11; Luke 3:21f.). Likewise it was the Spirit that furnished the motivating power for his ministry of liberation. In his synagogue speech at Nazareth he announced:

> The Spirit of the Lord is upon me,
> because he has anointed me to
>   preach good news to the poor.
> He has sent me to proclaim release
>   to the captives
> and recovering of sight to the blind,
> to set at liberty those who are
>   oppressed,
> to proclaim the acceptable year of the
>   Lord.
>   (Luke 4:18)

He then stated, "Today this scripture has been fulfilled in your hearing" (Luke 4:21). According to Matthew, Jesus' claim that the Kingdom of God had begun to invade earth in his exorcisms heightened itself still further when he asserted that he was casting out demons "by the Spirit of God" (Matt. 12:28; contrast Luke 11:20). We can feel the shock waves of this statement on Jesus' hearers when we realize that first-century Jews generally supposed that the Holy Spirit had departed from Israel with the last of the Old Testament prophets and would not reappear until the beginning of the messianic age. This teaching of Judaism, in combination with Joel's prophecy, impelled Luke to interpret what happened at Pentecost as the beginning of the "last days" (Acts 2:16f.). But Pentecost was truly only the beginning.[1] Early Christians came to expect that the Spirit would descend again and again, wherever they preached the message of Jesus. Paul wrote to the Corinthians:

> I decided to know nothing among you except Jesus Christ and him
> crucified. . . . And my speech and my message were not in plausible
> words of wisdom, but in demonstration of the Spirit and power.
>
> (I Cor. 2:2–4)

The word translated "power" in this passage *(dynamis)* is also one
of the Greek words for "miracle." Here it probably refers both to
the conversions which resulted from Paul's preaching and to what
he elsewhere calls "the signs of a true apostle . . . performed among
you in all patience, with signs and wonders and mighty works" (II
Cor. 12:12; see also Gal. 3:1–5). It was the Spirit that bestowed the
gift of faith (I Cor. 12:3); it was also the Spirit that enabled believers to work miracles *(dynameis;* I Cor. 12:10). According to John,
Jesus predicted that God's Spirit would convince the world of sin,
righteousness, and judgment, while at the same time guiding the
church into all truth (John 16:8–13). For the author of Hebrews,
this Spirit was the one that mediated to believers the powers *(dynameis)* of the coming age (Heb. 6:5). It is no exaggeration to
conclude that early Christians looked upon the Holy Spirit
as chief external Witness to the presence of Christ's reign.
Through the Spirit's work the world was coming to know its
Lord.

The Spirit also had a witnessing work to perform *within* believers. "He dwells with you," asserts the Johannine Jesus prior to his
resurrection, "and will be in you" (John 14:17). More than any
other New Testament author, Paul highlights this inner work of
the Spirit:

> Because you are sons, God has sent the Spirit of his Son into our
> hearts, crying, "Abba! Father!" (Gal. 4:6)

> Hope does not disappoint us, because God's love has been poured
> into our hearts through the Holy Spirit which has been given to us.
> (Rom. 5:5)

> But you are not in the flesh, you are in the Spirit, if the Spirit of God
> really dwells in you. Any one who does not have the Spirit of Christ
> does not belong to him. (Rom. 8:9f.)

When we cry, "Abba! Father!" it is the Spirit himself bearing witness with our spirit that we are children of God. (Rom. 8:15f.)

The Spirit's inner voice is "evidence" that we have been granted the gift of God's fatherly good favor. Elsewhere Paul calls the Spirit an *arrabōn,* a present pledge or down payment —one might even translate the word "engagement ring"—that we shall inherit future heavenly blessings (II Cor. 1:22; 5:5; see also Eph. 1:13f.). The Spirit constitutes the "first fruits," the initial blossoming of God's work to redeem the physical bodies of believers and transform the entire material world back into the perfection of Eden. The world longs for this glorious return to Paradise while believers, through the Spirit within them, can already begin to sense its dawning (Rom. 8:18–23). In both an exterior and interior manner, the Spirit discloses itself to New Testament believers as Mediator of God's new blessings in Christ. Through the Spirit, the gifts of the new creation enter human consciousness.

The Spirit as Gift Received, but Not Possessed

Is the Spirit itself a gift—or perhaps *The Gift?* Many New Testament passages seem to justify this terminology. According to Luke, Jesus taught:

What father among you, if his son asks for a fish, will instead of a fish give him a serpent; or if he asks for an egg, will give him a scorpion? If you then, who are evil, know how to give good gifts *(domata)* to your children, how much more will the heavenly Father give the Holy Spirit to those who ask him! (Luke 11:11–13; contrast Matt. 7:11, which has "good things" in place of "Holy Spirit")

On the Day of Pentecost, Peter urged the curious crowd that had gathered around the Spirit-filled disciples to

repent, and be baptized every one of you in the name of Jesus Christ for the forgiveness of your sins; and you shall receive the gift *(dōrea)* of the Holy Spirit. (Acts 2:38)

Later, Peter defended himself against conservative Jewish believers who had taken offense at his table fellowship with the uncircumcised Gentile Cornelius. Peter argued that it was perfectly right for him to act as he did because Cornelius and his people had received the Holy Spirit:

> As I began to speak, the Holy Spirit fell on them just as on us at the beginning. . . . If then God gave the same gift *(dōrea)* to them as he gave to us when we believed in the Lord Jesus Christ, who was I that I could withstand God? (Acts 11:15, 17)

Though Paul and John employ no noun for gift in connection with the Holy Spirit, they certainly imply that the Spirit is to be received as a gift.[2] Paul writes that God "has put his seal upon us and given us his Spirit in our hearts as a guarantee" *(arrabōn,* II Cor. 1:22; see also II Cor. 5:5). According to Rom. 5:5, "God's love has been poured into our hearts through the Holy Spirit which has been given to us" (see also Gal. 3:2, 5). In the Fourth Gospel, Jesus says, "I will pray the Father, and he will give you another Counselor to be with you for ever, even the Spirit of truth" (John 14:15). On the evening of the resurrection, when Jesus appears to his disciples behind closed doors, he breathes on them and fulfills this promise with the words: "Receive the Holy Spirit" (John 20:22). Finally, the writer to the Hebrews refers to those who have "tasted the heavenly gift *(dōrea),* and have become partakers of the Holy Spirit" (Heb. 6:4). If this sentence presents us with an example of Semitic parallelism—and that seems likely—then the heavenly gift is none other than God's Holy Spirit. We have good precedent, then, for understanding the Spirit as Chief Gift of the New Creation. The Spirit is the primal blessing which makes possible conversion and faith; through its activity every subsequent gift flows. "All [gifts] are inspired by one and the same Spirit, who apportions to each one individually as he wills." (I Cor. 12:11.)

While the Spirit somehow resides in individual believers, they in no sense have it at their disposal. The Spirit cannot be owned or contained by anyone, not even the corporate body of the church. It is more accurate to say that the Spirit possesses the church. It guides the church into truth (John 16:13). And it does this not only by comforting and nourishing the inner lives of believers but also by blowing where it wills (John 3:8), by opening and closing doors to the church's missionary efforts in the world (Acts 10:44ff.; 16:6ff.).

There is always more to the Spirit than any single believer or group of believers can comprehend. The disciples were "filled" with the Spirit on Pentecost (Acts 2:4), but they did not *possess* this fullness. Only a short time later, in a moment of great danger for the church, Luke reports that the Spirit had to fill them again so that they could speak the word of God with special boldness (Acts 4:23–31). The writer to the Ephesians knew that no believer could claim spiritual fullness as a stable or permanent condition. Precisely to those who had already received the Spirit at their baptism he wrote that they should keep on being

> filled with the Spirit [this is the sense of *plērousthe,* a Greek imperative in the present tense], addressing one another in psalms and hymns and spiritual songs, singing and making melody to the Lord with all your heart. (Eph. 5:18f.)

The Spirit always moves both within and without. The believer never has so much inside that more cannot enter. The Spirit remains Other; there is always more to meet, more to deal with and ponder, more to receive. It not only resides in believers but also moves in the world as it wills. Although it can be said that believers receive the Spirit, there is another sense in which it remains totally free, subject only to the will of God in Christ. The Spirit may be called a gift, but it is a gift which both surrounds and inhabits its recipients. Therefore, any claim to "possess" it must be understood in a very qualified way.

Holy Spirit and Human Spirit

Should we then think of the Spirit as an impersonal force, a wind (John 3:7f.) or fluid (John 7:38f.; Rom. 5:5) that takes over the believer and fills him or her up with its substance, thereby replacing the old self altogether? The frequent references in Acts to believers who are filled with the Spirit (Acts 2:4; 4:8, 31; 6:3, 5; 7:55; 9:17;

11:24) might seem to be leading us in this direction. So might Paul's quasi-mystical confession in Gal. 2:20: "I have been crucified with Christ; it is no longer I who live, but Christ who lives in me." In addition, we must take account of the apostle's view that praying in tongues constitutes a nonrational experience ("If I pray in a tongue, my spirit prays but my mind is unfruitful," I Cor. 14: 14). Paul's words might mean that exercising the gift of tongues requires an individual to become altogether possessed by the Spirit. This, after all, seems to have been what happened in the Old Testament stories about Samson, Saul, and others, who were literally taken over by the Spirit.

But in fact the New Testament texts cited above do not argue for possession. We have already noted that the writers of Acts and Ephesians conceive of spiritual fullness as a temporary condition which must be experienced repeatedly, and in part through human activity (keep on being "filled with the Spirit," Eph. 5:18). When Paul says that it is not he who lives but Christ within him, he immediately interprets his words to mean that "the life I now live in the flesh I live by faith in the Son of God . . ." (Gal. 2:20). Here it is *Paul* who lives, by responding to Christ in faith. This means that he retains a self after all. His living and believing are human activities, distinguishable from the Christ life within him. It is as if Paul feels that he has stepped too far into the realm of Hellenistic mysticism and must therefore assure the Galatians that he is not talking about total union with the Divine. As for praying in tongues, Paul urges the Corinthians to seek the gift of interpretation so that their nonrational experience can be supplemented with a rational one (I Cor. 14:13ff.). "What am I to do? I will pray with the spirit and I will pray with the mind also; I will sing with the spirit and I will sing with the mind also." (I Cor. 14:15.) While affirming the value of nonrational spiritual experiences (see I Cor. 14:4), the apostle opposes giving oneself over to ecstasy in public worship.[3] Paul rejects the notion that believers are powerless with regard to the activity of the Spirit within them. He urges Spirit-led prophets to postpone or even withhold their messages altogether when good order in the church seems threatened (I Cor. 14:29–33). On the other hand, to believers who seem in danger of forgetting their spiritual gifts, he writes, "Do not quench the Spirit, do not despise prophesying" (I Thess. 5:19). This advice, too, presupposes some form of human effort, along with that of the Spirit.

It seems best to conclude that God's Holy Spirit does not constitute the whole of the believer's inner life. It is a gift that works with —or against—the self. Two Pauline passages illustrate the proximity of self and Spirit, while at the same time maintaining a careful distinction between the two:

> When we cry, "Abba! Father!" it is the Spirit himself bearing witness with our spirit that we are children of God. (Rom. 8:15f.)

In this passage Paul describes the believer as one who has, or is, a spirit.[4] Elsewhere, the apostle refers to this element of the human makeup as the "inner man" (Rom. 7:22; II Cor. 4:16). It seems to be the core of existence, the self in humans with which the Holy Spirit can converse. According to Rom. 8:15f., the Holy Spirit joins the human spirit of a believer in its conviction that it is a child of God. The cry "Abba! Father!" thus issues from two inner witnesses, though it would be fruitless to ask what percentage of it is human and what percentage divine.

A second relevant passage occurs in Gal. 5:16f. There Paul writes:

> But I say, walk by the Spirit, and do not gratify the desires of the flesh. For the desires of the flesh are against the Spirit, and the desires of the Spirit are against the flesh; for these are opposed to each other, to prevent you from doing what you would. (Gal. 5:16f.)

Here the believer emerges as one who suffers from temptations to gratify the desires of the flesh, that is, the power of sin which still inhabits his or her body.[5] But the believer's self as such equals neither flesh nor Holy Spirit. It is rather that inner capacity for responding to the inclinations of flesh or Spirit. Here, as in Rom. 8:15f., the self must be considered a believer. In Galatians, Paul wishes to point up the vulnerability of the believing self. Since even the believer may succumb to the flesh's temptations ("The spirit indeed is willing, but the flesh is weak," Mark 14:38), the Holy

Spirit must protest against every leaning toward the flesh "in order that not whatever you want you might do these things" (a literal rendering of Gal. 5:17b). Paul recognizes that the desires even of the believing self remain ambivalent. Hence, believers must learn to listen for the true voice of the Spirit. This requires human attention, human effort.

Are we correct, then, in concluding that the ideal state of the believer would be one of cooperation between human spirit and Holy Spirit? Paul seems to suggest this when he urges his Philippian readers to "work out your own salvation with fear and trembling; for God is at work in you, both to will and to work for his good pleasure" (Phil. 2:12f.). Yet "cooperation" is probably not the right word, for Holy Spirit and human spirit are hardly equal partners. In other passages Paul speaks of walking by the Spirit or being led by the Spirit (Gal. 5:16, 18, 25; Rom. 8:4, 14). The image here is that of responding to the Spirit's direction in a manner analogous to the disciples' following after Jesus. If life in the Spirit means responding to the call "Follow me," we must reject the term "cooperation" as too egalitarian. Indeed, it would be wrong to understand even the best behavior of believers as the result of a fifty-fifty contract between their human spirits and the Holy Spirit. According to Paul, the desirable qualities of love, joy, peace, patience, kindness, goodness, faithfulness, gentleness, and self-control are best labeled "the fruit of the Spirit" (Gal. 5:22), not "fruits of our labors with the Lord." When believers respond, the Spirit will bloom in them, enriching them far more than their effort deserves. The Spirit is properly seen as God's foremost gift to believers because it both initiates (by its call) and completes (by its fruit) the working of God's will within them. Still, it never does so automatically or coercively. It accomplishes its purposes as all true gifts do, gently, by being received. The German neo-Pentecostal Arnold Bittlinger puts it nicely:

> The Spirit "speaks" and "helps." He never violates an individual, never attacks and destroys him, but rather brings the actual gifts

and potentialities of a person to full development . . . . He only works in a Christian to the extent that the Christian makes room for Him.[6]

The ways in which New Testament authors describe the Spirit's bestowal of itself—its nudgings and proddings and callings and longings—are almost innumerable. It will profit us, however, to look closely at some of the more prominent ones, reflecting on our own experiences of the Spirit as we go.[7] Above all, the Spirit is named as the one who enlivens. Thus, the Jesus of the Fourth Gospel describes God's Spirit as "rivers of living water" which bubble up inside a believer's heart (John 7:38f.). The Spirit refreshes humankind beyond the power of any oasis on earth. Jesus tells the Samaritan woman at Jacob's well:

> Every one who drinks of this water will thirst again, but whoever drinks of the water that I shall give him will never thirst; the water that I shall give him [the Spirit] will become in him a spring of water welling up to eternal life. (John 4:13f.)

Paul writes of the "law of the Spirit of life" which battles against "the law of sin and death" (Rom. 8:2). The Spirit not only *opposes* death, it actually triumphs over death in the very midst of death's domain, that is, in the human body.

> But if Christ is in you [through the Spirit], although your bodies are dead because of sin, the Spirit means life because of righteousness [a literal rendering of the Greek]. If the Spirit of him who raised Jesus from the dead dwells in you, he who raised Christ Jesus from the dead will give life to your mortal bodies also through his Spirit which dwells in you. . . . If you live according to the flesh you will die, but if by the Spirit you put to death the deeds of the [sin enslaved] body you will live. (Rom. 8:10–13)

The very presence of the Spirit means that death cannot finally defeat the human spirit. Even now, the Spirit offers itself to believers as a weapon in the fight against all death-serving powers. The author of life also becomes the means to prolong and enhance life. Lying defenseless and exhausted in the thick of battle, believers receive a cool drink of water and a sword. Both are the Spirit. The

Spirit enlivens believers by freeing them repeatedly from the kingdom of sin and death (Rom. 8:2). It does so by confirming in them their true identity as God's children, coheirs of God's glory along with Christ (Rom. 8:15–17). In the Spirit their lives penetrate beyond the decay and death which reign in the material world, though for the time being they must suffer along with creation under these alien forces (Rom. 8:18–23).

Like a soldier, the Spirit attacks sin, flesh, and death. A ferocious fighter, it will yield not an inch to the enemy (Gal. 5:16f.). Yet the Spirit never compels or overpowers believers. While it tolerates no sin, it bears with the weakness of the faithful, whose bodies are dead because of sin. It helps them with the most elementary of their responses to God: gifted as they are, they do not even know how to pray as they ought. "With sighs too deep for words," the Spirit communicates to God what believers want and need to say, but cannot because of their human limitations (Rom. 8:26f.). Far from lifting them out of everyday life to heaven, the Spirit sensitizes them to their role in the longing of created matter for redemption, thus inducing both dissatisfaction with the *status quo* and at the same time fashioning within them the patience to endure that comes with hope (Rom. 8:22–25). The Spirit is truly empathic. It knows the suffering of those weakened by sin and stands by them in their distress. But it also leads them on, quietly, beyond whatever gifts and tasks they currently think themselves capable of accepting. The Spirit will not let believers stand still for long. Through its ministrations God works mightily to strengthen each one's "inner man" (Eph. 3:16). Such strength does not, however, manifest itself in the form of brute force. As the Spirit's leading comes gently, so does the "strong" behavior exhibited by those whom the Spirit guides. Paul writes to the Galatians:

> If we live by the Spirit, let us also walk by the Spirit. Let us have no self-conceit, no provoking of one another, no envy of one another.
>
> Brethren, if a man is overtaken in any trespass, you who are spiritual *(pneumatikoi)* should restore him in a spirit of gentleness. Look to yourself, lest you too be tempted. Bear one another's burdens, and so fulfil the law of Christ. (Gal. 5:25 to 6:2)

Humility characterizes the lives of those led by the Spirit, for they know how weak they are and how much they depend on the Spirit's gracious perseverance within them.

We can perhaps sum up (but by no means comprehend) the Holy Spirit's ministry to the human spirit of believers in the words of I Cor. 12:11: "All these [gifts] are inspired by one and the same Spirit, who apportions to each one . . . as he wills." The gifts referred to are those described in I Cor., chs. 12 to 14. We shall give them closer attention in Chapter 4. But this passage also strains to be interpreted more broadly. For even when the gifts of tongues, healing, prophecy, etc., do not come into view, the New Testament teaches that the Spirit's intention for each believer is to actualize itself in that person as a gift tailored specifically to his or her needs within the plan of God. Sometimes the Spirit takes the form of a familiar gift, a word of comfort or exhortation that one recognizes as necessary for his or her well-being in faith. More often, the Spirit's urgings come to believers in ways they have never before experienced: some new person or crisis, some color of reality they have never seen before; a call to action that they would never have thought of themselves, or, had they thought of it, they would have resisted it as foolish.[8] Such novelty often seems more disturbing than comforting, but that makes it no less gracious. For the Holy Spirit is a living, pulsating, changing Gift which always seeks to bestow itself anew to the human spirit of believers: "God is at work in you, both to will and to work for his good pleasure" (Phil. 2:13).

The Corporate Thrust of the Spirit

In the passage above, the word for "you" is plural. While Paul and his New Testament colleagues affirm that the Spirit acts within believers as individuals, they also make it quite clear that this activity has been granted for the sake of the believing community, the church. Whatever private satisfaction Christians may derive from the Spirit's life within them is to be overshadowed by the joy of participation in the Spirit's "collective" work of strengthening and expanding the church. "To each is given the manifestation of the Spirit *for the common good,*" Paul reminds the Corinthians (I Cor. 12:7, italics added). This simple point needs to be written in boldface type today when so many are rushing to actualize their potential for no other reason than that of personal aggrandizement.[9]

We shall have more to say below about how gifts granted to individuals find their proper fulfillment in service to church and world. Here we are concerned to show that for New Testament Christians the Holy Spirit was understood as a blessing bestowed primarily for the sake of the church's mission. When the Johannine Jesus calls God's promised Spirit "another Counselor" (John 14: 16f.; the Greek word is *paraklētos,* from which the English "Paraclete" is formed), he is not talking about a comfort that will come to particular believers in times of illness, personal crisis, etc. Rather, he means the Spirit's lawsuit against an unbelieving world. *Paraklētos* is a legal term that means something close to our contemporary "defense attorney." In this role the Spirit confronts a hostile, accusing world through the church's message: "When he comes, he will convince the world concerning sin and righteousness and judgment" (John 16:8; see also John 14:16f.). It follows that when Jesus, in this same section of John's Gospel, refers to the Spirit as teacher (John 14:26), witness (John 15:26f.), and guide to truth (John 16:13ff.), he intends to highlight the Spirit's corporate work through the church. By nature the Spirit is a missionary who works to extend Christ's rule over all creation. Whatever personal strength and comfort believers receive from the Spirit must flow into this cosmic venture.

In Acts, Luke seems most insistent upon portraying mission as the chief activity of the Spirit. Ironically, this book, which speaks so often of Christians being filled with the Spirit (outside of Acts, only Eph. 5:18 uses this terminology!), tells us little about how such an experience felt.[10] The reason for Luke's silence on this matter is clear. He forgoes writing a psychology of the Spirit because what interests him far more is the *external* work of the Spirit in church and world. The spiritual filling of individual believers serves this end. On Pentecost the tongues in which the Spirit-filled disciples speak are foreign languages that allow them to proclaim to an international audience "the mighty works of God" (Acts 2:11) so that all can repent and be baptized (Acts 2:38). Luke represents Pentecost as the first installment in the actualizing of Jesus' ascension promise:

> You shall receive power when the Holy Spirit has come upon you; and you shall be my witnesses in Jerusalem and in all Judea and Samaria and to the end of the earth. (Acts 1:8)

As the church's mission unfolds, so does the fulfillment of this prophecy. Over and over Luke shows us how the Spirit fills specific people, not for their private edification but for their role in the corporate task of witnessing to Christ (see Acts 4:8, 31; 9:15–17; 11:23f.; and the preaching activities of the Spirit-filled "deacons" Stephen and Philip in Acts 6:3 to 8:40).[11]

Consistent with his stress upon the world-directed activity of the Spirit is Luke's narration of certain key moments in the early church's history. At these special turning points the Spirit discloses itself to initiate or direct the young movement's missionary work. Here are three examples:

> Now in the church at Antioch there were prophets and teachers, Barnabas, Symeon who was called Niger, Lucius of Cyrene, Manaen a member of the court of Herod the tetrarch, and Saul. While they were worshiping the Lord and fasting, the Holy Spirit said, "Set apart for me Barnabas and Saul for the work to which I have called them". (Acts 13:1f.)

> And they [Paul and Timothy] went through the region of Phrygia and Galatia, having been forbidden by the Holy Spirit to speak the word in Asia. And when they had come opposite Mysia, they attempted to go into Bithynia, but the Spirit of Jesus did not allow them. (Acts 16:6f.)

> Now after these events Paul resolved in the Spirit to pass through Macedonia and Achaia and go to Jerusalem, saying, "After I have been there, I must also see Rome." (Acts 19:21)

It was not always easy for the church to agree upon the direction in which the Spirit was leading. The story of the apostolic council at Jerusalem, called to decide whether Gentile believers needed to be circumcised, makes this clear. Nevertheless, once the issue at hand had been debated by the apostles and elders, a resolution offered by James found speedy acceptance. According to Luke, what happened was neither an executive decision nor a democratic one. It was simply a common understanding which "seemed good to the Holy Spirit and to us" (Acts 15:28). One might call the council's decision a pneumatic consensus. We contemporary Christians who have suffered through long, frustrating meetings of church councils and sessions may stand in awe at the smoothness of this process. In fact, we may register some doubt that Luke has told us the whole truth about the course of the discussion. In any event, we find confirmation for the view that Luke wants to impress upon us the massive degree to which the Spirit takes charge over the church's corporate missionary effort. In God's campaign against the powers of darkness the Spirit reveals itself not only as living water and a weapon for each soldier but also as field marshal who draws up and issues the comprehensive battle plan. Corporately as well as individually, the Spirit gives itself constantly to believers, thus revealing itself as the primal life force in God's New Creation.

Other Spirits

New Testament believers knew that the Spirit whose presence gave them life was not the only spirit at work in their world. Yet for them, the Holy Spirit stood out as qualitatively superior to all the other pneumatic phenomena of their day. How do the New Testament writers talk about the difference between the Holy Spirit and other spirits? On the basis of what we now know about the first-century world from extra-Biblical sources, how well does their claim stand up?

Most easily distinguishable from the Holy Spirit are those evil spirits which were thought to cause madness and other illnesses. The Gerasene "demoniac" who was healed by Jesus is a case in point. So completely possessed was he by an unclean spirit that he broke his restraining chains and screamed incessantly, all the while abusing himself with stones. Even his speech had fallen under the control of the alien spirit (Mark 5:1–20 and parallels). We find a similar example in the epileptic boy whom Jesus encounters following his descent from the mountain of the transfiguration. Describing the boy's illness in first-century terms, his father tells Jesus:

> Teacher, I brought my son to you, for he has a dumb spirit; and wherever it seizes him, it dashes him down; and he foams and grinds his teeth and becomes rigid. (Mark 9:17f.)

An equally violent possession is narrated in Acts, ch. 19:

> Some . . . itinerant Jewish exorcists undertook to pronounce the name of the Lord Jesus over those who had evil spirits, saying, "I adjure you by the Jesus whom Paul preaches." Seven sons of a Jewish high priest named Sceva were doing this. But the evil spirit answered them, "Jesus I know, and Paul I know; but who are you?" And the man in whom the evil spirit was leaped on them, mastered all of them, and overpowered them, so that they fled out of that house naked and wounded. (Acts 19:13–16)

Other evil spirits were manifest in idolatry, blasphemous speech, or false prophecy. Paul refers to at least two of these phenomena when he tells the Corinthians:

> You know how, in the days when you were still pagan, you would be seized by some power which drove you to those dumb heathen gods. For this reason I must impress upon you that no one who says "A curse on Jesus!" can be speaking under the influence of the Spirit of God. (I Cor. 12:2–3 in the NEB alternate translation)

Here Paul reminds the Corinthians of the ecstatic worship which they had formerly practiced, perhaps in union with the temple prostitutes of Aphrodite, whose cult flourished in Corinth during the first century.[12] The curse on Jesus to which Paul refers was probably not hypothetical, but a real occurrence in the Corinthian congregation. It might have been the outcry of a Christian prophet under the influence of an unknown force.[13] Similar spirit-induced proclamations are treated by the author of I John under the rubric of false prophecy. The elder warns his readers not to

> believe every spirit, but test the spirits to see whether they are of God; for many false prophets have gone out into the world. By this you know the Spirit of God; every spirit which confesses that Jesus

Christ has come in the flesh is of God, and every spirit which does not confess Jesus is not of God. (I John 4:1–3; see also Matt. 7: 21–23)

All the pneumatic phenomena described above have one feature in common: an evil spirit appears to be manipulating its human prey, usually in a violent physical way so that the person can no longer control his or her emotions, thoughts, and actions. Presumably, the human spirit of the person possessed has little awareness of its own bizarre behavior, its consciousness having been captured by the alien spirit.

We know about this sort of possession also from records of pagan religious practices in the Hellenistic era. Lucian of Samosata (A.D. 120–180) provides an eyewitness account of the worship of the Syrian goddess at Hieropolis. He describes it as a brutal orgy induced by a "frenzy." According to his report, the ceremony reached its climax when the *galli*, the eunuch priests of the goddess, danced madly about, inflicting gashes and lashes on their fellow priests as well as on themselves. At this point male onlookers sometimes experienced such a powerful urge to worship the goddess that they castrated themselves on the spot in order to join the ranks of the *galli*.[14] A similar account comes to us from the second-century author Lucius Apuleius. One of the *galli* he watched raved "as if some divine spirit filled him" and uttered "violent prophecies."[15] We know that the cult of this Syrian goddess existed in Rome prior to and during the first century.[16]

The long succession of priestesses *(pythiae)* who proclaimed the oracles of the Greek god Apollo at Delphi, just north of Corinth on the Greek mainland, represents yet another example of spirit possession. The oracle at Delphi existed long before the Christian era and was reported to be functioning well into the second century A.D. Hellenistic believers like Paul certainly knew about it. Eyewitnesses reported that when the *pneuma* of Apollo entered into the priestess, she panted violently and uttered ecstatic speech, her hair streaming as if blown by the wind. Devotees understood that the voice with which she spoke was that of the divine Apollo.[17] Sometimes, however, a spirit other than Apollo's came upon the priestess, with terrifying results. In his book *The Greeks and the Irra-*

tional, Eric Dodds calls attention to a passage from Plutarch (A.D. 50–120) in which the ancient author passes along an eyewitness story of such a tragedy at Delphi.[18] Plutarch writes:

> Now what happened to the *pythia* [on that day]? She descended into the place of the trance only with apprehension and reluctance. From her first responses it was evident by her hoarse voice that she was not recovering from her trouble and that she resembled a driven vessel, filled with a dumb and evil wind *(pneuma).* Finally, totally distressed, she threw herself toward the exit, rushing with a strange and terrible cry and putting to flight not only the seers but also the prophet Nicander and the devotees of the god who were present. A few minutes later when they entered, they picked her up, her senses restored. But she survived only a few days. (*On the Disappearance of Oracles,* 438b)[19]

The ancients knew that ecstasy was risky business. Still, it must have been widely experienced (or at least simulated) in the first century. The Greek-speaking Jew, Philo of Alexandria, a contemporary of Paul, wrote against the professional diviners of his day who claimed to interpret portents, auguries, and sacrificial entrails under the influence of a prophetic spirit. Philo denounces these people as charlatans, charging that their practice is really "a corruption of art, a counterfeit of the divine and prophetic possession." He then goes on to describe what he understands to be authentic prophecy:

> No pronouncement of a prophet is ever his own; he is an interpreter prompted by Another in all his utterances, when knowing not what he does he is filled with inspiration, as the reason withdraws, and surrenders the citadel of the soul to a new visitor and tenant, the Divine Spirit which plays upon the vocal organism and dictates words which clearly express its prophetic message. (*Special Laws,* IV, 48f.)

Philo probably formulated this definition not from tradition alone —he does not seem to be alluding to any particular passage from the Old Testament—but also from personal experience. He may have had in mind the ecstatic singing and dancing of a first-century Jewish ascetic community called the Therapeutae which he witnessed and described in a work called *The Contemplative Life* (see esp. sections 83–90). These people appear to have sung their spiritual songs in the vernacular, not in unknown tongues.

Pneumatic phenomena, both positive and negative, abounded in the ancient Hellenistic world, as the cited examples show. The possessed individual experienced a loss of ordinary selfhood. An entering spirit literally took over the mental and physical processes so that little or no sense of control remained.[20]

Was the Spirit which we Christians call Holy experienced differently by New Testament believers? In one sense the answer must be an unequivocal yes. Without exception New Testament writers affirm that the Holy Spirit always testifies to the Lordship of Jesus (I Cor. 12:3; John, chs. 14 to 17; I John 4:1ff.). But from here on the answer to our question becomes more difficult, for there are events recorded in the New Testament which might have been understood by contemporary eyewitnesses as cases of spirit possession. Pentecost is one of them. We have no information about the consciousness of those early believers who were moved to speak in foreign languages as the Spirit gave them utterance (Acts 2:4). Were they aware of what they were doing and saying? Were they actively following the Spirit's guidance, or were they altogether taken over by the Spirit? We cannot tell from Luke's account. All we can say is that some of the bystanders thought the speakers were drunk (Acts 2:13), which suggests that they appeared to be not in full command of their faculties. Paul anticipates a similar advent of the Spirit when he asks the Corinthians, "If therefore the whole church assembles and all speak in tongues, and outsiders or unbelievers enter, will they not say that you are mad?" (I Cor. 14:23). In each of these cases the New Testament writers presuppose that speaking under the Spirit's influence might look to observers like a loss of control on the part of the participants. Thus Paul takes pains to show that while the Holy Spirit may manifest itself in ways that seem indistinguishable from certain types of Hellenistic ecstasy, its true self emerges most characteristically in a more sober manner, especially through intelligible prophecy (see I Cor., ch. 14). Paul agrees with Philo that the divine Spirit speaks "words which clearly express its prophetic message." But he parts company from his Jewish contemporary by interpreting the Holy Spirit's action within believers as something less than possession.

For Paul, the practice of all spiritual gifts, including tongue-speaking and prophecy, involves a measure of free will. Tongue-speaking, in fact, seems to be almost totally under the control of the individual; otherwise, Paul's counsel to practice it privately or to limit its congregational use to two or three persons in the presence of an interpreter makes no sense (see I Cor. 14:27f.). With prophecy, the impulse to speak appears to come altogether from the Spirit. Yet it too differs from possession, since, like tongues, it can be restricted to a few occurrences per service of worship (I Cor. 14:29f.). When one prophecy interrupts another, the first prophet can yield to the new revelation with a minimum of confusion. "The spirits of prophets are subject to prophets." (I Cor. 14:32.) This apparently means that the urging of the Spirit can be resisted, in fact *should* sometimes be resisted, for the sake of decency, peace, and good order (I Cor. 14:31ff., 39f.).

In sharp contrast to most of the pneumatic phenomena known to us from the Hellenistic world, the Holy Spirit works gently. Coercion and violence are not its customary mode of operation. Even the quasi-ecstatic behavior seems unusually "controlled" by Hellenistic standards. Consistent with this observation is the virtual absence of references in the New Testament to Spirit-inspired dancing, jumping, quivering, falling, or similar bodily movements.[21]

In summary, we can say that over against the first-century environment God's Holy Spirit appears to be quite distinctive, if not absolutely unique.[22] The distinctiveness shows itself in two ways. First, the Holy Spirit always speaks for and witnesses to Jesus as the Christ. Second, spiritually filled believers and the spiritually guided church are allowed a larger measure of conscious control over their behavior than the possessing spirits of the Hellenistic age permit. To put it in the familiar language of our discussion, the Holy Spirit does not force itself upon a recipient; nor does it simply take over a person or group when it is received. True to form, the Spirit always presents itself as a gift.

The Giver Draws Near in the Gift

The gift of the Spirit proves to be even more magnificent than it seems initially. It is actually the supreme pledge that Almighty God himself has drawn near with his mercy. Already during his ministry Jesus interpreted the Spirit's activity in his healings as a sign of God's nearness. To those who accused him of working in league with Satan he countered:

> If I cast out demons by Beelzebul, by whom do your sons cast them out? Therefore they shall be your judges. But if it is by the Spirit of God that I cast out demons, then the kingdom of God has come upon you. (Matt. 12:27f.; a parallel passage in Luke 11:20 has "finger" in place of "Spirit")

According to the Johannine Jesus, God's bestowal of the Spirit means that when "a man loves me, he will keep my word, and my Father will love him, and we will come to him and make our home with him" (John 14:23). The Spirit's residence within believers creates a hospitable heart that allows them to welcome Jesus and the Father, to be at home with God. The familiar apostolic benediction—"the grace of our Lord Jesus Christ, the love of God, and the communion of the Holy Spirit be with you"—may be understood in a similar light. Communion *(koinōnia)* is the Spirit's work within us that enables us to receive Christ's grace and the Father's love. As Paul puts it in Rom. 5:5: "God's love has been poured into our hearts through the Holy Spirit which has been given to us." The writer to the Ephesians highlights this nearness to God in declaring that all believers have "access in one Spirit to the Father" (Eph. 2:18). Through Christ's reconciling work the Spirit opens up a door for us to the Father. We become sons and daughters in his family, living in the very same house with him:

> So then you are no longer strangers and sojourners, but you are ... members of the household of God, built upon the foundation of the apostles and prophets, Christ Jesus himself being the cornerstone, in whom the whole structure is joined together and grows into

a holy temple in the Lord; in whom you also are built into it for a
dwelling place of God in the Spirit. (Eph. 2:19–22)

Ordinarily, the New Testament writers, like their Old Testament
counterparts, take great care to preserve God's transcendence.
Thus, they generally refrain from speaking of the Father's residence within us. Ephesians 2:22 represents a bold departure from
this tradition when it asserts that in the Spirit the corporate body
of believers becomes a dwelling place for God. But the writer of
I John takes this claim even farther:

If we love one another, God abides in us and his love is perfected
in us.
    By this we know that we abide in him and he in us, because he
has given us of his own Spirit. . . . Whoever confesses that Jesus is
the Son of God, God abides in him, and he in God. (I John 4:12–15)

For this writer, even the individual believer, inspired by the Spirit
to confess Jesus' divine Sonship and empowered to love the brethren, becomes a dwelling place for God the Father. No doubt the
authors of Ephesians and I John would have denied that the Spirit's
presence produced a divine-human *union.* They were too Jewish
for that. They knew that only in the age to come would God be
"all in all" (I Cor. 15:28). The Spirit remained for them a distinction as well as a link between heaven and earth. Nevertheless, we
cannot fail to be impressed by the almost mystical quality of their
words. They were God-intoxicated believers, awakened by the
Spirit to discern the Father's presence where they had not sensed
it before.

    In this they were simply following out a line of experience
common to the New Testament as a whole. Wherever the Spirit
appears, the transcendent God becomes more discernible. The
Holy Spirit is no momentary thrill. It comes to us as nothing less
than the God of Abraham, Isaac, and Jacob, whose fountain of life
sustains all creation. In the Spirit, the Father of Jesus Christ and
Giver of every good and perfect gift (James 1:17) draws near to
become Our Father. To speak of "spiritual" gifts, therefore, means
to speak of gifts that sensitize us anew to the power and love of God
for us.

CHAPTER 4

Renewal and Service Through Charismata

In his Spirit, God draws near as Giver. Or perhaps we should say that through the Spirit, God invites us to open up, to perceive the nearness of his gifts and accept them. For God is at hand even when we fail to notice him. Insofar as we are enabled to sense them through the Spirit, we can properly think of all God's gifts as spiritual, even the ones that seem most material: food, clothing, shelter, etc. Our look at the Old Testament has already confirmed that.

The New Testament, however, singles out special gifts disclosed through the Spirit. Sometimes these are called charismata. Paul says that "there are varieties of gifts *(charismata),* but the same Spirit" (I Cor. 12:4). It is important to note that "spiritual" gifts can also be thought of as originating with Jesus or God the Father (I Cor. 12:5f.). The old theologians were right in affirming that there is no "division of labor" in the Trinity. If Paul in I Cor., ch. 12, tends to link charismata most closely with the Spirit, that is probably because he wishes to argue from where the Corinthians are. They lean toward interpreting their experience of the risen Christ primarily in terms of *pneuma* (I Cor. 2:6 to 3:3; 14:37; 15:45). Paul attempts to show them that the spiritual fullness in which they exalt carries with it a heavy weight of responsibility (see esp. I Cor. 4:8 to 6:20 and Chapter 2). Therefore he stresses that the manifestation of the Spirit granted to each believer comes "for the common good" (I Cor. 12:7). All gifts, he says, are inspired and distributed by the Spirit primarily to equip Christ's body for mutual service (I Cor. 12:8–26).

What are the special gifts called charismata, and what makes them so special? We shall devote our attention to these two questions in the present chapter. When participants in current movements for spiritual renewal confront such questions, they generally appeal to the four major "lists" of charismata found in I Cor., chs. 12 to 14; Rom. 12:6ff.; Eph. 4:7ff.; and I Peter 4:10f. The reader is urged to examine these passages before proceeding.

Among the charismata mentioned in I Cor., ch. 12, are prophecy, wisdom, knowledge, extraordinary faith, discernment, healing and the working of other miracles, speaking in tongues and its interpretation, and the communal tasks of helping and administration (I Cor. 12:4–11, 27–30).[1] The most detailed treatment of charismata in the entire New Testament is found in I Cor., chs. 12 to 14. As such, it is often taken to be "normative" for charismatic self-understanding and practice today. The gifts Paul discusses there are held by many to be the most important ones; indeed, they are seen by Pentecostal believers as absolutely essential for mature Christian living.[2] This view finds some support in Paul's admonition to his Corinthian readers that they "earnestly desire the spiritual gifts *(pneumatika),* especially that [they] may prophesy" (I Cor. 14:1).

But we must resist using I Cor., chs. 12 to 14, normatively in a *limiting sense.* In Rom. 12:6ff., written just a year or so later, Paul also labels as charismata such activities as ministerial serving *(diakonia),* exhorting or encouraging others, contributing money, lending a hand, and performing acts of mercy. The only charisma repeated per se from the Corinthian list is prophecy. The fact that it occurs first in Rom. 12:6 and takes precedence over other gifts in I Cor. 14:1 witnesses to its great importance for Paul (see also I Peter 4:10). As a group, however, the other activities described in Rom., ch. 12, do not seem nearly so spectacular by current standards as the gifts cataloged in I Cor., ch. 12. Probably they would have been harder for outsiders to identify as "special" disclosures of the Spirit.

The list in Eph. 4:7ff. adds a further note of complexity. Although the Greek word *charisma* does not appear, the idea of special gifts from the risen Christ certainly does. Here the gifts are people:

> "When he [Christ] ascended on high he led
>   a host of captives,
>   and he gave gifts to men."

> ... And his gifts were that some should be apostles, some prophets, some evangelists, some pastors and teachers. (Eph. 4:8, 11)

The officeholders referred to in this passage overlap to a degree with the activities and people detailed in I Cor., ch. 12, and Rom., ch. 12, but there is no one-to-one correspondence. When thinking about gifts, the New Testament writers do not appear to be striving for rigid definitions.

The fourth list, in I Peter, hardly constitutes a list at all, for it mentions only two charismatic tasks:

> As each has received a gift *(charisma),* employ it for one another, as good stewards of God's varied grace: whoever speaks [i.e., prophesies], as one who utters oracles of God; whoever renders service, as one who renders it by the strength which God supplies. ... (I Peter 4:10f.)

In summary, the evidence suggests that if we want to work out a comprehensive New Testament understanding of charismata, we shall have to broaden our vision beyond the popular lists. After taking a panoramic view, we can return to the data reflected in these four passages with a sense of perspective.

An Overview of Charismatic Phenomena in the New Testament

The word *charisma* occurs seventeen times in the New Testament, only once outside the letters traditionally ascribed to Paul (Rom. 1:11; 5:15, 16; 6:23; 11:29; 12:6; I Cor. 1:7; 7:7; 12:4, 9, 28, 30, 31; II Cor. 1:11; I Tim. 4:14; II Tim. 1:6; I Peter 4:10). We should not, however, conclude that Paul is an eccentric on the subject. We know that the phenomena behind the word were quite widespread in the early church. We have already noted how profoundly gifted the early church felt itself to be, and how frequently it acknowledged the Spirit as chief mediator of this giftedness. Divine gifts were felt to abound, whether believers explicitly named them as *charismata* or not. The element of God's free grace in these gifts comes to light in the prominence of the *char* stem words: "joy" *(chara)*, "rejoicing" *(chairō)*, "thanksgiving" *(eucharisteō* and *eucharistia)*, "bestowing" *(charizomai)*, and of course "grace" itself *(charis)*. These brothers, sisters, and cousins of *charisma* occur scores of times in the New Testament, usually in connection with God's gifts.

Most of the charismatic gifts described in Paul's letters appear also in the narratives of Luke-Acts, even though the word *charisma* is never used. In Luke's writings we find examples of prophecy (Luke 1:67–79; 2:25–38; Acts 2:14–21; 11:27f.; 13:1; 15:32; 19:6f.; 21:8–10), speaking in tongues (Acts 2:1ff.; 10:44ff.; 19:6f.), healing (Acts 3:1–10; 5:14f.; 9:17f., 32-34; 14:8ff.; 16:16ff.; 28:8ff.), exhortation and encouragement (Acts 11:23; 13:43; 14:22; 15:32; 16:40; 18:27; 20:1f.; 27:34ff.), miracles (Acts 6:8; 8:6ff.), teaching (Acts 2:42; 4:2; 5:21, 25, 28, 42; 11:26; 13:1; 15:35; 18:11, 25; 20:20; 28:31), discernment (Acts 5:3f.; 8:18–21; 13:9ff.), and administration (Acts 14:23; 15:13ff.).

The charismatic phenomena of prophecy and miracles as events in the church's life are also alluded to in John 14:12; I John 4:1ff.; Heb. 6:5; James 5:13ff.; and Rev. 2:1ff.; 10:7; 11:18; 16:6; 18:20, 24. In fact, John the Revelator understands his entire book as a prophetic message granted him through a series of visions (Rev. 22:6ff.). Finally, even apart from the passages in which he uses the word *charisma*, Paul makes clear references to Christian prophecy (I Thess. 2:15; 5:19; II Thess. 2:2) and the working of miracles in connection with his preaching (Rom. 15:19; I Cor. 2:4; II Cor. 12:12; Gal. 3:5). The Pauline author of Ephesians considers Christian prophets foundational to the church (Eph. 2:20). He urges his readers to keep on being "filled with the Spirit, addressing one another in psalms and hymns and spiritual songs, singing and making melody to the Lord with all your heart" (Eph. 5:18f.; see also Col. 3:16). We conclude, then, that the phenomena Paul calls *charismata* abounded in the early church. They were "normal" experiences for nearly all the Christians who wrote and first read the New Testament.

Nevertheless, Paul's reflections upon the charismata turn out to be most useful, because he is the only New Testament author who does in fact *reflect* upon them. He does not simply report or recommend them. He tries to evaluate them, to understand what role they ought to play in the life of the church, to rank them in order of importance. It may be that he himself hit upon the name *charisma* as he attempted to make sense out of these spiritual gifts.[3] With his great sensitivity to God's grace *(charis),* he would certainly have inclined toward a name derived from the *char* stem. As he traveled from congregation to congregation in the ancient world, Paul witnessed the full range of early Christian experience. And of course he had plenty of his own. Much of his writing consists of attempts to order and articulate this new spirituality in the light of his Jewish heritage. Paul will be our chief teacher as we continue to explore the meaning of the charismata. And so we turn to those passages in which he deals explicitly with them.

The apostle occasionally uses the word *charisma* in quite a general way. The famous maxim in Rom. 6:23 serves as an illustration: "For the wages of sin is death, but the free gift of God *(charisma)* is eternal life in Christ Jesus our Lord." Usually eternal life has a future connotation in Paul. It is something we inherit after death. That is probably the meaning in this passage as well (see Rom. 6:22). Yet when Paul uses *charisma* one chapter earlier in Rom., ch. 5, it obviously refers to a gift *presently* enjoyed by Christians:

> But the free gift *(charisma)* is not like the trespass. For if many died through one man's trespass, much more have the grace of God and the free gift in the grace of that one man Jesus Christ abounded for many. And the free gift is not like the effect of that one man's sin. For the judgment following one trespass brought condemnation, but the free gift *(charisma)* following many trespasses brings justification. (Rom. 5:15f.)

Here Paul is talking about the righteousness through faith granted to all Christians by God's grace. These two texts from Romans show the fluidity of Paul's thought. For him, charismata can be both present and future. Moreover, he obviously thinks of all Christians as "charismatics," since all have received God's righteousness and all therefore have become heirs of eternal life. This same view emerges in a later passage where the Pauline author of

II Timothy identifies the charisma of God not with a special talent but with the Holy Spirit which is granted to every believer (II Tim. 1:6f., 14).

Most occurrences of the word *charisma,* however, do point to specific gifts or disclosures of the Spirit which are not bestowed on all believers equally. One group of passages shows that *charisma* can mean a concrete gift of encouragement, release, or (probably) healing. Paul writes to the Romans:

> I long to see you, that I may impart to you some spiritual gift *(charisma pneumatikon)* to strengthen you, that is, that we may be mutually encouraged by each other's faith, both yours and mine. (Rom. 1:11f.)

Paul probably looks forward to an informal exchange of enlivening talk with the Roman congregation. He may have in mind the transmission of specific gifts, such as prophecy and discernment, to certain individuals. At any rate, the emphasis is upon the refreshing effect of the gift.

In II Corinthians, Paul applies the word *charisma* to a recent personal experience:

> We do not want you to be ignorant, brethren, of the affliction we experienced in Asia; for we were so utterly, unbearably crushed that we despaired of life itself. Why, we felt that we had received the sentence of death; but that was to make us rely not on ourselves but on God who raises the dead; he delivered us from so deadly a peril, and he will deliver us; on him we have set our hope that he will deliver us again. You also must help us by prayer, so that many will give thanks on our behalf for the blessing *(charisma)* granted us in answer to many prayers. (II Cor. 1:8–11)

Paul appears to be narrating his unexpected (miraculous?) release from an oppressive imprisonment which had carried with it the probability of the death sentence. This deliverance, granted him by God "in answer to many prayers," he sees fit to call a charisma.

The experience of speaking in tongues probably fits into this same category of charismata. Those who practice the gift report a dramatic sense of release, refreshment, and relaxation; and this squares with Paul's view that "he who speaks in a tongue edifies [builds up] himself" (I Cor. 14:4). With tongues the charisma is not a one-time event but a more or less constant possibility.[4]

In the phrase "gifts *(charismata)* of healing" (I Cor. 12:9, 28, 30) we encounter a certain ambiguity. Is Paul talking about gifts given to healers or to those healed?[5] David DuPlessis, well-known Pentecostal minister and writer, takes the second position:

> They are gifts of healing which the sick receive—not the evangelist or pastor. For example, we call a fellow a milkman, but all he does is deliver milk. He gets it from the dairy and delivers it to those who have ordered. . . . So the healer delivers to the sick what the Holy Spirit gives.[6]

DuPlessis' position finds support in the fact that there is no New Testament evidence for an *office* of healers in the early church. The stress throughout lies on the gifts of healing received from God through the Spirit by those in need, not on the human mediators of the gifts or the people who pray as intercessors. The charismata of encouragement, release, and healing seem to fall into a natural grouping. We can, without being judgmental, call them gifts passively received. They come, like nourishment, to those whose lives need renewing. At the time of their reception these charismata do not contain within themselves specific directives for ministry.

But there are other charismata, most of them in fact, which do exactly that. Romans, ch. 12, is a good place to begin our examination of this category:

> For as in one body we have many members, and all the members do not have the same function, so we, though many are one body in Christ, and individually members one of another. Having gifts *(charismata)* that differ according to the grace *(charis)* given to us, let us use them: if prophecy, in proportion to our faith; if service, in our serving; he who teaches, in his teaching; he who exhorts, in his exhortation; he who contributes, in liberality; he who gives aid, with zeal; he who does acts of mercy, with cheerfulness. (Rom. 12: 4–8)

The chief point here is that charismata are not to be neglected, since God bestows them precisely for ministry. He intends them to be used generously in service to other Christians and, almost certainly, to non-Christians as well (see Gal. 6:1–10). Paul would probably shudder at being compared with our contemporary human potential movements. But the two have this much in common: they both assume that people need encouragement to use the gifts which are already theirs. For Paul, that use must be ministry. As we learned in Chapter 3, the Spirit leads and nudges, but never compels a person to act against his or her deepest sense of what is right. In the same way its charismata constitute no replacement for human effort. We can think of them as promises, empowerings, calls, or certifications for ministry. But the ministry itself requires picking up the gift and putting it to work. This urging to use one's charisma for ministry appears again in I Timothy where the author exhorts his young friend to

> attend to the public reading of scripture, to preaching, to teaching. Do not neglect the gift *(charisma)* you have, which was given to you by prophetic utterance when the elders laid their hands upon you. (I Tim. 4:13f.)

Probably we are to think of Timothy's ordination as a bishop or deacon, during which a Christian prophet pronounced some special blessing for ministry upon him. It may surprise us that such impressive charismatic gifts for ministry as those granted to the Roman congregation and Timothy could be allowed to fall into disuse. But the New Testament is quite realistic about our sloth. It seems universally human to forget about God's blessings, no matter how spectacular they are. Pentecostal Christians today report that they can all too easily cease speaking in tongues or prophesying and return to their old patterns of living.

There is another reason why Paul and the author of I Timothy insist so strongly upon putting charismata to use in ministry, namely, the tragic *misuse* of charismata in the Corinthian congregation (see Chapter 2). Paul and his apostolic followers were especially sensitive to such dangers. They did not wish to see the Corinthian problems repeated in the lives of other Christians. As a congregation, the Corinthians suffered no charismatic deficiency. Paul tells them that they "are not lacking in any spiritual gift" *(charisma;* I Cor. 1:7). All types of charismata appeared in their worship service (see I Cor., chs. 12 to 14). Nevertheless, when it came to employing their gifts according to God's will, the Corinthians turned out to be "babes in Christ" (I Cor. 3:1–3). One big problem in Corinth seems to have been that believers with certain types of gifts (we do not know which) looked down upon their brothers and sisters with other gifts. Paul offers as a corrective a discourse on the necessity of interdependence within Christ's body. He writes:

> There are many parts, yet one body. The eye cannot say to the hand, "I have no need of you," nor again the head to the feet, "I have no need of you." On the contrary, the parts of the body which seem to be weaker are indispensable. (I Cor. 12:20–22)

On the other hand, believers made to feel shortchanged with their charismata by the proud suffered from discouragement. Apparently, some had even begun to ask whether they belonged in the church at all. No doubt they also envied the gifts of the proud. To them, Paul writes:

> If the foot should say, "Because I am not a hand, I do not belong to the body," that would not make it any less a part of the body. And if the ear should say, "Because I am not an eye, I do not belong to the body," that would not make it any less a part of the body. If the whole body were an eye, where would be the hearing? If the whole body were an ear, where would be the sense of smell? But as it is, God arranged the organs in the body, each one of them as he chose. (I Cor. 12:15–18)

Paul believes that through the Spirit, God is always distributing charismata to a Christian congregation (see I Cor. 12:11) in such a way as to maximize its potential for harmony and mutual ministry:

> God has so adjusted the body, giving the greater honor to the inferior part, that there may be no discord in the body, but that the members may have the same care for one another. If one

member suffers, all suffer together; if one member is honored, all rejoice together. (I Cor. 12:24–26)

This means that not everyone can have every gift (I Cor. 12:28–30). Nor does the ideal functioning of a congregation simply happen on its own. It requires love (I Cor., ch. 13), a mature understanding of priorities in charismatic practice (I Cor. 14:1, 20), and a sense of good order (vs. 27ff., 40). Obedience and plain hard work are presupposed.

In I Cor. 7:7, Paul reveals an unusual ministerial charisma of his own. In the course of giving advice to married couples in Corinth he appears almost overwhelmed by the complexities of conjugal life. He exclaims, "I wish that all were as I myself am" (that is, single; see I Cor. 7:8). But as soon as he has blurted this out, he thinks better of it. He concedes: "But each has his own special gift *(charisma)* from God, one of one kind and one of another." The interesting point here is that Paul can conceive of his celibacy, and perhaps marriage too, as a charisma.[7] Today we tend to think of our marital status as a matter of personal choice or fate, but not as a spiritual gift. Paul refrains from telling us in so many words why he chooses to call his single state a charisma. Probably it has much to do with his conception of himself as a unique apostle of Christ (see I Cor. 15:9–10). Did Paul receive his charisma of celibacy at the time of his call to apostleship? Or did it dawn on him later, perhaps via revelation (see Gal. 2:2; II Cor. 12:1), that his single state was a gift of God for ministry? The second possibility has much in its favor, for we know from II Cor. 1:8ff. that he was open to the discovery of new charismata in the course of his apostolic work.

It would be going too far to conclude that Paul tended to name everything that enhanced his ministry a charisma. Yet we can detect in Rom. 8:32 an almost cosmic breadth in his expectations for appearances of God's grace in the lives of believers. There he writes, "He [God] who did not spare his own Son but gave him up for us all, will he not also give us [*charisetai* literally means, "bestow upon as a gracious gift"] all things with him?" The impression we receive is that for Paul many hidden charismata were waiting eagerly to become visible. He had obviously not closed the door to discoveries of new spiritual gifts, especially when they appeared as fresh empowerings for ministry.

The Pauline writer to the Ephesians names apostles, prophets, evangelists, pastors, and teachers as Christ's gifts *(domata)* to the church (Eph. 4:8–11). Undoubtedly Paul would have agreed. Yet the apostle himself never applies the word *charisma* to people, not even to church leaders. The nearest he comes is in I Cor. 12:28, but a literal translation shows that even here he refrains from equating the two:

> And [these] God has placed in the church: first apostles, second prophets, third teachers, then miracles, then charismata of healing, helpful deeds, administrative acts, various kinds of tongues.

After listing the three chief officeholders in the church, Paul then switches from people to activities. Technically, only the latter can be called charismata (see I Cor. 12:9–10). Apparently Paul wants to make sure that his readers understand the difference between people and the spiritual gifts granted to them. The gift is not the person; therefore no one can glory in it as if it were a personal accomplishment, a deserved payment for outstanding piety or services rendered. In chiding the Corinthians for just such a pride, he writes: "For who sees anything different in you? What have you that you did not receive? If then you received it, why do you boast as if it were not a gift?" (I Cor. 4:7). Even apostles must admit to being nothing more than fragile pots into which God pours his transcendent power (II Cor. 4:7ff.). Paul was chosen despite the fact that he was morally unworthy (I Cor. 15:7ff.).

Nevertheless, having made this point, Paul is quite willing to affirm that on specific occasions, certain people may be experienced by others as a grace *(charis)*. He writes to the Corinthians that had he been able to carry out his planned itinerary (he was not), he would have visited them twice in the course of one missionary journey, thus granting them a double *charis* (II Cor. 1:15f.). Another time Paul writes to the householder Philemon from prison, asking him to prepare a guest room, for, as he puts it, "I am hoping through your prayers to be granted [*charisthēsomai* means "bestowed as a gracious gift"] to you" (Philemon 22).

Charismata and the Natural Order

Paul's open-ended talk about charismata raises the question of how "supernatural" they are.[8] In contemporary charismatic movements great emphasis is placed upon dramatic prophecies, healings, and speaking in tongues. As a result many Christians who do not participate in these movements may easily get the impression that insiders draw a heavy line between human talents and temperaments, which they regard as natural gifts, and the wholly supernatural gifts of the Spirit. Such a distinction prompts legitimate objections. Can we really tell whether Paul's charisma of celibacy was altogether a supernatural gift and not also a matter of personal inclination? Again, how important is it to speak of the charismata of liberal contribution or administration (Rom. 12:8; I Cor. 12:28) as direct interventions of God *rather than* human acts of good stewardship?

At least two writers who identify with charismatic movements, both of them well acquainted with the New Testament evidence, recognize the difficulties inherent in making such sharp distinctions. The English Pentecostal leader Donald Gee insists that spiritual gifts are always something supernatural added to natural talents and preferences. Nevertheless he challenges the view, common in his circles, that such gifts must be "a hundred per cent miraculous" and therefore easy to discern.[9] For Gee, the mark of a true spiritual gift is that it makes the presence of the Holy Spirit evident in meetings of Christian congregations (I Cor. 12:7). Hence, it does not matter whether the gift comes across as spectacular or whether it appears rather subdued, as in an edifying word of knowledge or wisdom. The decisive test is that the emergence of the gift must result in the explicit worship of God (I Cor. 14: 20).[10] Gee holds that "the bestowal of a spiritual gift does not imply an ability to use it at the will of a recipient."[11] Yet he also wants to maintain that gifts such as knowledge and wisdom appear from time to time in the regular preaching or teaching of an individual. They appear in activities ordinarily initiated by human will and dependent to some degree upon the training of human ability. Moreover, Gee notes that one often receives gifts of the Spirit during the willed activities of study or meditation.[12] The effect of this interpretation of spiritual gifts is to blur the line between natural and supernatural, or as Gee puts it, "to enlarge our conception of [the] truly supernatural life," so that it includes activities and practices customarily taken to be quite ordinary.[13]

In reflecting upon how to evaluate ministries of preaching and teaching that seem particularly full of blessing, Gee asks whether we should labor to discern in them a spiritual gift or "Pentecostal plus." His answer summarizes his major hypothesis:

> We have come to the borderline between the natural and the supernatural, and it is a fallacy to imagine that it is easily drawn. We may wish it could be so, but we must accept the truth. . . . To value as we ought the precious quality of divine inspiration in all the gifts of the Spirit, while at the same time we recognize the inescapable human element in them, is the mark of being well instructed in the truth.[14]

Gee's answer to the question of whether charismata are natural or supernatural speaks to those who operate comfortably with such categories. It remains true to Paul insofar as it intends to expand the realm of the "supernatural" beyond the spectacular. But we must keep in mind that Paul himself never uses the words "natural" and "supernatural" as such. Instead, he prefers to speak of "psychic" *(psychikos)* and "spiritual" *(pneumatikos)* as the two possible modes of experiencing reality (I Cor. 2:10–16). For Paul, the psychic person is not one who, as we might suspect, enjoys clairvoyant powers. Rather, he or she is one who relies solely on the resources of human wisdom. A pneumatic person, on the other hand, has found his or her understanding enlarged to discern the Holy Spirit at work where others cannot. We encounter here a *type* of natural-supernatural distinction, yet it applies not to the spiritual gifts themselves but to a person's ability to perceive and accept them.

> The unspiritual man *(psychikos)* does not receive the gifts of the Spirit of God, for they are folly to him, and he is not able to understand them because they are spiritually discerned. The spiritual man judges [or discerns] all things. (I Cor. 2:14f.)

For Paul, "all things" are potential gifts of the Spirit (see Rom. 8: 32). The apostle does not seem to care whether we label a given event, act, or talent natural or supernatural. He is far more concerned about whether the Spirit's working can be recognized in it and acknowledged.

A German neo-Pentecostal author who recognizes the problem of drawing distinctions between natural and supernatural gifts is Arnold Bittlinger. He concludes that Paul simply does not differentiate between the two.[15] For Bittlinger, a charisma is that gift manifested when "being set free by the Holy Spirit, my natural endowments blossom forth glorifying Christ and building up His church."[16] This definition seems consistent with Paul's discussion of spiritual gifts in I Cor., chs. 12 to 14. But Bittlinger may go beyond the apostle's teaching when he asserts:

> There is no Christian action that is independent of the Holy Spirit. In practical terms this means, for example, that for the Christian doctor his total activity is charismatic activity. A prescription or an inoculation are only different ways of laying on hands. Both are done prayerfully and in fellowship with Jesus.[17]

It is questionable whether Paul would have agreed with this global description of charismatic activity. It seems to allow no *specific* moments for acknowledging the Spirit's presence. Probably the apostle would say that while a believer's entire life—apart from lapses into rebellion against God—may be construed as charismatic, some moments are more charismatic than others. Thus Paul does not refrain from ranking spiritual gifts. Some, he frankly states, must be considered superior to others; they are "higher" *(meizona)* charismata, which should be especially sought after by believers (I Cor. 12:31).

What are these higher gifts? Apparently they constitute a group of charismata called *pneumatika*, spiritual charisms (I Cor. 14:1; Rom. 1:11). Of course, all charismata are spiritual insofar as they all emanate from the Holy Spirit (I Cor. 12:4). But the *pneumatika* seem to be gifts through which the Spirit's presence becomes unusually real to the assembled congregation. E. E. Ellis is probably right in calling them "gifts of inspired perception, verbal proclamation and/or its interpretation."[18] In I Cor., chs. 12 to 14, Paul wants to instruct his readers in the proper use of these *pneumatika* (I Cor. 12:1). Tongue-speaking is clearly one of them, but within this category it forms the bottom rung of the ladder (I Cor. 14:1ff.), for although it edifies the person who practices it, it does not, unless interpreted, aid the congregation (vs. 4, 13f.). The key property of the *pneumatikon* is that it enables a community of Christians to acknowledge, articulate, and praise God's presence among them. For this reason prophecy turns out to be chief among the *pneumatika* (I Cor. 14:1–5). It speaks the deep truths of God in plain language to everyone present, thus producing the maximum amount of edification (I Cor. 14:3f.). Presumably, utterances of wisdom and knowledge (I Cor. 12:8), as well as hymns, lessons, and revelations (I Cor. 14:26), also fall into the category of the *pneumatika*. They too are experienced as inspired messages, granted by the Spirit at particular moments for the whole congregation to hear. It may be that Paul thinks of the last three as forms of prophecy, for they appear to be used interchangeably with the word *prophēteia* in I Cor. 14:24–33.[19] Utterances of wisdom and knowledge, however, must be distinguished from prophecy (I Cor. 12:8–10). We should probably think of them as short, epigrammatic sayings inserted spontaneously into the church's worship, but without the claim, "Thus says the Lord." As we noted above, Gee believes that they can occur during the ordinary activities of preaching and teaching. Paul would surely have held out the possibility that any member of the congregation might speak them.

Pneumatika, then, are charismata meant to be practiced within the context of congregational worship. They appear for a particular moment in whomever the Spirit selects (I Cor. 12:11). Not even prophecy, the noblest of them, can be restricted to that group of church leaders who hold the office of prophet (I Cor. 14:26–33). These greater charismata are democratic and temporary. No person can boast if the Spirit chooses him or her to practice one of them during a service of worship. Nor should a believer count on "owning" such a *pneumatikon* in the sense of expecting to reproduce it at will in some future gathering of the congregation. We cannot tell whether these higher charismata should be called natural or supernatural. A word of wisdom might be spoken by a simple or a learned person. A hymn might be sung to the congregation by a skilled musician or by someone with no training whatsoever. While these offerings *could* vary in eloquence or melodic quality in direct proportion to the natural talents of the individual, aesthetic criteria would not be ultimate in determining whether or not they revealed God's presence to the congregation. As always, charismata are "spiritually discerned" (I Cor. 2:14).

Individuation and Incorporation Through Charismata

We have just said that no believer should expect to repeat a given *pneumatikon* at will from one service of worship to the next. This statement can stand as long as we place our emphasis upon the words "at will," but it needs to be amplified if we are to understand Paul's teaching about charismata more fully.

The apostle makes it clear that some charismata, at least, come to individuals as long-term gifts which can be recognized by others as a regular or continuous feature of that person's Christian identity. Thus Paul writes that "each [believer] has his own special gift from God *(hekastos idion echei charisma),* one of one kind and one of another" (I Cor. 7:7). Paul's special gift is his celibacy. Others, he knows, have different gifts which characterize their everyday life-styles. Within the worship service itself certain individuals were probably associated with the practice of certain gifts. Otherwise, Paul's counsel to be neither proud of one's spiritual gifts as superior nor despairing of them as inferior (I Cor. 12:14–26) makes little sense. It seems likely that within given congregations some people were expected to do most of the prophesying, others most of the hymn-composing, others most of the interpretation of tongues, etc.

There would be then an element of regularity about the distribution of charismata to individuals. We can even go so far as to say that the charismata a believer "has" for a long period of time, or those which are repeatedly given to that person, play a large role in defining his or her Christian identity. This identity by means of gift can be called individuation.[20] Paul writes: "All these [charismata] are inspired by one and the same Spirit, who apportions to each one individually as he wills" (I Cor. 12:11). It is as if the Spirit approaches a person and says, "Through the gift(s) which I bestow upon you I am making you different from all others and setting you apart for my special purposes" (see Acts 13:1-3). The uniqueness experienced by charismatically gifted individuals was (and is) most liberating. It means concrete assurance that each believer counts as a person before God. The gift becomes a pledge that this person has an essential role to play in God's plan, a place that no one else can fill. In the individuation process believers become convinced that God wants to use them as they are. They need not strive to change in order to be acceptable. Paul experienced individuation at the time of his call to apostleship:

> Last of all, as to one untimely born, he [Christ] appeared also to me. For I am the least of the apostles, unfit to be called an apostle, because I persecuted the church of God. But by the grace of God I am what I am, and his grace toward me was not in vain. On the contrary, I worked harder than any of them, though it was not I, but the grace of God which is with me. (I Cor. 15:8-10)

By individuating believers through the bestowal of charismata, God reveals his sovereign freedom. The church would never have chosen its own persecutor as chief apostle to the Gentiles, but God did. Sometimes God's humor shines through in the way he distinguishes individuals through his gifts. A friend of mine feels certain that one of his charismata is the ability to find parking places; and as far as I can tell, he is right. That gift may seem trivial—hardly a mark of spirituality by traditional standards—but like other "small" charismata it turns out to be eminently useful for the mission of the Christian community.

Charismata enable believers to see themselves as valuable individuals, quite apart from the expectations placed upon them by others. Still, their proper sense of self-worth dare not result in proud isolation from the community of believers. This was the danger in Corinth, and so Paul writes, "To each is given the manifestation of the Spirit *for the common good*" (I Cor. 12:7, italics added). The charisma serves to shape an individual Christian's identity, but it does so in order to prepare that person for service to others. John Schütz says it well:

> [The charisma] trims and bounds the ego of the religious man. If in the body every member's contribution is counted worthy and must be honored because all men, possessing the spirit, manifest that spirit in individual gifts, nevertheless, this sense of individuation does not give license to individualism. Quite the contrary. By stressing individuation Paul rescues the self from submersion in a principle like pneuma, where self and spirit become indistinguishable. So the self is not only trimmed and bounded, but extended. The self is submerged only in the larger body where it does not lose, but finally gains its true identity.[21]

The body to which Schütz refers is the body of Christ, the church. It can be no accident that in the very chapter where Paul lists the widest variety of spiritual gifts given to individuals, he moves on immediately to sketch his view of the optimal Christian community. The same Spirit which individuates through the charismata also incorporates the charismatic person into the church to fulfill his larger purposes (I Cor. 12:12f.). Paradoxically, through the communal giving and receiving of spiritual gifts, both individual and corporate identities flourish, with the result that a fluid, power-charged unity begins to surge through the congregation.

The Transmission of Charismata

How *are* spiritual gifts given and received? Here we run up against a question hotly debated in the church today. Classical Pentecostals, as well as neo-Pentecostals within the main-line churches, generally believe that to enjoy the charismata described in I Cor., ch. 12, or Rom., ch. 12, one must first experience a dramatic baptism in the Spirit. Evidence for such a baptism is taken to be one's ability to speak in tongues. Tongue-speaking thus becomes, for all practical purposes, the indispensable rite of passage to a superior level of spirituality. Unless one receives and practices glossolalia, advancement to the "higher gifts" of knowledge, interpretation, and prophecy is not deemed likely.[22] Presumably, Christians who take this position would accept without difficulty the Biblical evidence that Paul's broad definition of charisma includes spiritual gifts not listed in I Cor., ch. 12, and Rom., ch. 12 (see, for example, Rom. 5:15, 16; 11:29; I Cor. 7:7; II Cor. 1: 11). They would probably grant the title "charismatic" to any believer who claims to have found eternal life in Christ (Rom. 6: 23). But the classical Pentecostal and neo-Pentecostal positions tend to part ways from more traditional theology by insisting that only through a baptism in or release of the Holy Spirit[23] does one qualify to receive the full array of spiritual gifts. This is usually understood to follow sometime after water baptism. As we examine the various New Testament witnesses concerning the reception of charismata, we shall keep this question before us: Is there one particular spiritual event or charisma that one must experience as a doorway to the "higher gifts"?

At least one passage suggests that early Christians understood gifts of the Spirit to be connected with water baptism. In the Pentecost story, Peter, newly gifted with a tongue of fire and the ability to speak in foreign languages, tells the perplexed Jerusalem crowd: "Repent, and be baptized every one of you . . . for the forgiveness of your sins; and you shall receive the gift of the Holy Spirit" (Acts 2:38). As noted earlier, the gift of the Holy Spirit probably refers to the Spirit itself. In the light of the context we must suspect that Luke thought of the Spirit's coming as visible through signs in the new believers, just as it was a few moments earlier in Peter and the other disciples. This hypothesis finds support in the story of some Samaritan believers who, though baptized in Jesus' name, had not yet received the Holy Spirit (Acts 8:14ff.). The deficiency was regarded by believers in Jerusalem apostles as an exception to the general rule that the Spirit comes along with water baptism.[24] So it happens that Peter and John, after praying for the Samaritans, lay hands upon them, with the result that they do finally receive the Spirit. Luke does not state that the apostles transmitted the Spirit from themselves to the Samaritans by the laying on of hands, though Simon Magus, witnessing the event, interprets it in just this way. He covets for himself what he takes as their extraordinary power. This probably means that in Luke's opinion Simon saw some dramatic behavioral change in the Samaritan believers once they had received the Spirit. Whether this was speaking in tongues or some other charisma we cannot tell. In any event, these two passages from Acts support the view that according to Luke's understanding of the early church's experience, charismata ordinarily came to believers with or shortly after water baptism.[25]

Yet the arrival of charismata was never understood by New Testament writers to have ceased with water baptism. Paul's letters clearly show that these gifts would appear periodically in a believer's life as part of his or her growth in faith (e.g., I Cor. 14:1ff.; II Cor. 1:11; Rom. 1:11). One way in which individuals could receive them was through the person's positive response to a specific spoken word of the gospel. Paul tells the Romans, whom he has never met:

> I long to see you, that I may impart to you some spiritual gift
> *(charisma pneumatikon)* to strengthen you, that is, that we may be
> mutually encouraged by each other's faith, both yours and mine.
> (Rom. 1:11f.)

What the apostle envisions here is not his preaching as a missionary before the congregation. It is, rather, informal Christian conversation in which both he and the Romans can speak about their faith, so that all can become mediators of spiritual gifts.[26] Interestingly, Paul, a veteran proclaimer of the gospel, expects to *receive* a spiritual gift through the Romans. Conscious of standing near the end of his ministry in Asia Minor and the Balkans (Rom. 15:18f.), he knows he is not at the end of his growth in grace. Despite the glowing expectation that he will come to the Romans from Jerusalem "in the fulness of the blessing of Christ" (Rom. 15:29), he still wants to gain, spiritually, from these younger, less experienced believers.

Another Pauline witness to the ongoing reception of spiritual gifts through the word appears in Gal. 3:5. The apostle asks his readers, "Does he who supplies the Spirit to you and works miracles among you do so by works of the law [implied answer: no] or by hearing with faith [implied answer: yes]?" The spoken word, when greeted with faith, serves as a channel for the bestowal of charismata.

Romans 12:1ff. should be understood in this vein. In Rom., chs. 9 to 11, Paul sketched the mysterious plan through which God is working to unite Jews with Gentiles under his gracious reign. Paul now urges his hearers to praise God for his inscrutable mercies by offering up their bodies to him as "a living sacrifice" so that they may be "transformed" by the renewal of their minds and thus "prove what is the will of God" (Rom. 12:1-2). What happens is that those who keep giving themselves up to God in this way—the present tenses used throughout indicate repeated action—receive new insight into their special place within the congregation. In other words, they are granted clearer visions of which charismata they possess and how these gifts should be put to use. Paul tells the Romans that with a renewed mind they can

> think [about themselves] with sober judgment, each according to the measure of faith which God has assigned him. For as in one body we have many members, and all the members do not have the same function, so we, though many, are one body in Christ, and individually, members of one another. Having gifts *(charismata)* that differ according to the grace given to us, let us use them. (Rom. 12:3-6)

In this passage the charismata are seen as already present in the congregation. The Romans "have" them (v. 6). And yet, through this new response to God's word of mercy, the charismata will, in effect, be given again, for now they can be understood in a deeper manner.[27] Possibilities and limitations will become more sharply defined in the minds of individual believers, with the result that a richer interdependence can take place in the congregation.

Three passages in the New Testament affirm that a courageous defense of the gospel in the face of great opposition will be granted to believers as a charisma. A word of Jesus states this plainly:

> When they bring you to trial and deliver you up, do not be anxious beforehand what you are to say; but say whatever is given to you

in that hour, for it is not you who speak, but the Holy Spirit. (Mark 13:11; see also Matt. 10:19f. and Luke 21:14f.)

This promise finds a double fulfillment in the book of Acts: first, when the apostles are commanded by the Jerusalem authorities not to preach about Jesus publicly (Acts 4:17f.) but then find themselves refilled with the Holy Spirit to speak the word of God boldly (Acts 2:4; 4:23–31); and second, when Stephen receives extraordinary wisdom through the Spirit to refute Jewish arguments against Jesus' Messiahship in the synagogue of the Freedmen (Acts 6:8–10). In these passages a particular gift is understood to be always available when Christians suffer duress from civil authorities. Krister Stendahl aptly observes that "the Christian before the courts is the only one to whom the Scriptures promise . . . a special gift of the Spirit".[28] No such promise exists, for example, in connection with speaking in tongues. But when Christians must give an apology for their faith in straightforward language before the unbelieving powers of this age, they can be sure of receiving a charisma.

So far we have been discussing gifts that believers receive as a result of someone else's initiative: the offer of baptism from a preacher, the spoken word of another, and the Spirit's direct intervention through Christian testimonies before the authorities. We have already discovered that believers themselves can do something about receiving spiritual gifts. Paul says that they are to "seek" or "earnestly desire" the higher charismata, especially prophecy (I Cor. 12:31; 14:1). This seeking is not to be for self-aggrandizement. Rather, as I Cor., ch. 14, shows, it will be an expression of the believer's need to be better equipped for ministry within the congregation.

There are two ways of seeking charismata. One, not surprisingly, is prayer. Thus Paul writes that "he who speaks in a tongue should pray for the power to interpret [it]" (I Cor. 14:13). Perhaps remembering Jesus' promise that the Spirit would help them make a good confession before the Jewish council, the Jerusalem apostles pray: "Grant to thy servants to speak thy word with all boldness, while thou stretchest out thy hand to heal, and signs and wonders are performed through the name of thy holy servant Jesus" (Acts

4:29f.). Immediately, Luke reports, "the place in which they were gathered together was shaken; and they were all filled with the Holy Spirit and spoke the word of God with boldness" (Acts 4:31). Later, the prayer for healings, signs, and wonders also receives a positive answer (Acts 5:12–16). Such events appear to have been forecast in a saying of Jesus recorded by Luke:

> Ask, and it will be given you; seek, and you will find; knock, and it will be opened to you. For every one who asks receives, and he who seeks, finds, and to him who knocks it will be opened. What father among you, if his son asks for a fish, will instead of a fish give him a serpent; or if he asks for an egg, will give him a scorpion? If you then, who are evil, know how to give good gifts to your children, how much more will the heavenly Father give the Holy Spirit to those who ask him! (Luke 11:9–13)[29]

Jesus does not say that believers will always receive just the gift they request, only that in God's answer there will come some manifestation of the Spirit which constitutes a "finding." On the other hand, it seems that one need not pray a specifically petition-ary prayer in order to receive spiritual gifts. According to Acts 13: 1ff., the prophets and teachers of the church in Antioch "were worshiping God and fasting" when the Holy Spirit directed them (through prophecy?) to set apart two of their number, Saul and Barnabas, for a missionary journey. The practice of fasting suggests that the group was seeking divine guidance, but we find no indica-tion in the text that they were praying for a charisma.

The New Testament also teaches that it is possible to seek the Spirit or one of its gifts for others through intercessory prayer. Upon learning that the new believers in Samaria had not received the Spirit at their baptism, Peter and John "came down [to Sa-maria] and prayed for them that they might receive the Holy Spirit" (Acts 8:15). The Pauline writer to the Colossians assures his readers that he has "not ceased to pray for you, asking that you may be filled with the knowledge of [God's] will in all spiritual wisdom and understanding" (Col. 1:9; see also Phil. 1:9). Paul himself speaks of an intercessory prayer that has led to the be-stowal of a charisma—in this case, his own. In II Cor. 1:11 he calls his unexpected deliverance (probably from prison) a "blessing *(charisma)* granted us in answer to many prayers." C. K. Barrett's translation of II Cor. 1:10–11, which correctly interprets the verses in their context, makes clear that the "many prayers" were not limited to Paul's own:

> It is God who rescued us from so threatening a death, and will rescue us, God in whom we have set our hope; and he will yet deliver us if you too cooperate on our behalf by your prayer, in order that from many people thanks may be rendered to God on our behalf for the gift of grace *(charisma)* bestowed on us through the agency of many.[30]

Here the apostle receives a charisma through the prayers of believers to whom he has ministered—not a bad model for relationships between ministers and recipients of ministry today. Gifts may flow from God to his commissioned and ordained servants precisely through those who stand most in need of their service. In this we see a reciprocity altogether characteristic of God's lively grace.

But we have said that there are two ways of seeking a spiritual gift. If the first is prayer, the second can best be described as loving action. Paul closes the twelfth chapter of I Corinthians with these words:

> Are all apostles? Are all prophets? Are all teachers? Do all work miracles? Do all possess gifts of healing? Do all speak with tongues? Do all interpret? [implied answer: no] But earnestly desire the higher gifts *(charismata)*.
>
> And I will show you a still more excellent way. (I Cor. 12:29–31)

This "more excellent way" is none other than love, introduced by Paul in the now famous thirteenth chapter of I Corinthians:

> If I speak in the tongues of men and of angels, but have not love, I am a noisy gong or a clanging cymbal. And if I have prophetic powers, and understand all mysteries and all knowledge, and if I have all faith, so as to remove mountains, but have not love, I am nothing. If I give away all I have, and if I deliver my body to be burned, but have not love, I gain nothing. . . . Love never ends; as

for prophecies, they will pass away; as for tongues, they will cease; as for knowledge, it will pass away. For our knowledge is imperfect and our prophecy is imperfect. (I Cor. 13:1–3; 8–9)

Even the highest charismata become worthless displays of egotism unless they are guided by love into serving others. Enduring love is the right "way" to use spiritual gifts because it puts them in true perspective. Ultimately, it is not the gifts themselves that count, valuable as they are, but the love toward others for which they equip believers. That is why Paul, having sung his ode to love, begins ch. 14 with the words: "Pursue *(diōkete)* love and desire *(zēloute)* the spiritual gifts" (author's translation). The first Greek word is the stronger of the two. Paul wants to tell the congregation that in seeking spiritual gifts, they ought to spend most of their mental and physical energy attempting to love their neighbors. The Corinthians have shown themselves "eager for manifestations of the Spirit" (I Cor. 14:12), but mostly, it seems, in order to build themselves up and distinguish themselves from their neighbors (see I Cor. 12:20ff.; 14:4, 26ff.). In twentieth-century language we might say that they were developing their individual spiritual potentials in competition with their brother and sister believers.

Paul chides the congregation for its chaotic worship in which all members clamor to practice their spiritual gifts aloud at the same time (I Cor. 14:23–26). This display, he says, may benefit the individuals involved, but in corporate worship it proves selfish and foolish, since it does not help the rest of the congregation (I Cor. 14:1–11). The twist in Paul's argument comes at v. 12: "You are, I know, eager for gifts of the Spirit; then aspire above all to excel in those which build up the church" (NEB). In effect, Paul is telling the Corinthians that if they will sincerely attempt to strengthen one another, disclosures of the Spirit equal to that task will follow (especially prophecy). Zeal for the church's health leads to prayer for gifts (I Cor. 14:13) but is, in a sense, prior to it and separable from it. The "more excellent way" of loving intent plus loving action shapes prayers so that they conform to God's will. Focusing on the neighbor's needs rather than on one's own desire for spiritual advancement becomes, ironically, a powerful means of advancing spiritually (see Mark 4:24f.).

Since he calls love a fruit of the Spirit (Gal. 5:22), Paul would no doubt say that even the inclination to love comes as a gift of God's grace (see I Cor. 15:10). Yet it is a gift that requires human effort for its actualization. Psychologically, one experiences it as the overcoming of inertia, as work, even as risk. At the time Paul wrote II Cor., ch. 9, he sensed a fear in his readers that if they responded to his appeal for money to meet the needs of poor Christians in Jerusalem, they would lack sufficient resources for themselves (a familiar refrain in contemporary churches). To overcome their resistance, Paul reminded them of God's extraordinary economy:

> Remember: sparse sowing, sparse reaping; sow bountifully, and you will reap bountifully. . . . It is in God's power to provide you richly with every good gift *(charis);* thus you will have ample means in yourselves to meet each and every situation, with enough and to spare for every good cause. . . . Now he who provides seed for sowing and bread for food will provide the seed for you to sow; he will multiply it and swell the harvest of your benevolence, and you will always be rich enough to be generous. (II Cor. 9:6–11, NEB)

In Rom. 12:8 this liberal giving of money is understood as a charisma; II Cor. 9:6ff. makes the additional point that the gift may not be consciously experienced as one's own until one actually practices it. Sometimes, Paul says, we must act out of a conviction that God is magnanimous, even though we do not feel particularly gifted. Everything depends upon our view of God. Is he stingy or generous? If the latter, we can love daringly, trusting that he will bestow—the future tense is to be taken literally—the necessary charismata.

Spiritual gifts, then, may be received through water baptism, a faithful response to the spoken word, the Spirit's speech in the apology of believers on trial, and through seeking by means of prayer or loving action. But there is still another perspective on the transmission of charismata, one we have already encountered in the Old Testament. In a way, it encompasses all the other modes. It can best be called God's sovereign freedom to give charismata when and how he pleases. Quite apart from human desire, will, and effort, God can bestow (or withhold) his gifts. "All [gifts] are inspired by one and the same Spirit, who apportions to each one individually as he wills." (I Cor. 12:11.) Finally, it is God alone who chooses which gifts we are to receive and the manner of their reception. Thus Paul can confess that even Israel, despite its general rejection of Jesus' Messiahship, is and will remain a charismatic people by virtue of God's ancient election (Rom. 11:28–29).

Within the history of the church the event of Pentecost clearly demonstrates God's gift-giving sovereignty. Although Luke states that the apostles and their companions were praying prior to the Spirit's descent (Acts 1:14), he never suggests that the charismata they manifested at Pentecost came as a result of their prayer. According to his account, the promise of the Spirit had already been made before it entered the apostles' minds to request it (Luke 24:49; Acts 1:5, 8). This charismatic bestowal constituted a phase of God's providential plan which none could either withstand or hasten. Paul's conversion and reception of the Spirit are also understood by Luke as God's sovereign act (Acts, ch. 9; see also Gal. 1: 15). Following Paul's jarring encounter with Christ on the road to Damascus, Ananias, a believer residing in the city, is commanded by God in a vision to heal and baptize his persecutor. Ananias resists this call but eventually, in the tradition of Moses and the Old Testament prophets, carries out his task after all:

> So Ananias departed and entered the house. And laying his hands on him he said, "Brother Saul, the Lord Jesus who appeared to you on the road by which you came, has sent me that you may regain your sight and be filled with the Holy Spirit." And immediately something like scales fell from his eyes and he regained his sight. Then he rose and was baptized, and took food and was strengthened. (Acts 9:17–19)

The implication is that Saul received a charisma of healing through the laying on of hands. We cannot tell from the text whether he was filled with the Spirit prior to, along with, or soon after baptism. But clearly the Prime Mover behind all these steps of his reception into the church was God alone.

Similarly, it is God who controls the affairs of believers in Samaria. They were properly water-baptized in Jesus' name and—

as far as we can tell—not at all deficient in faith. Still they failed to receive the gift of the Spirit. According to Luke, God chooses *in this case* to bestow the Spirit through the agency of Peter and John by means of prayer and the laying on of hands (Acts 8:12–17). In contrast (but again through God's sovereign intervention), the Gentile household of Cornelius receives charismata prior to any praying or touching on the part of Peter (Acts, ch. 10). In fact, these new believers begin to speak in tongues even before they have made a profession of faith in Christ. Or rather, their speaking in tongues, which Luke portrays as language "extolling God" (Acts 10:46), constitutes their profession of faith.

We suggested above that Paul's charisma for celibacy might have grown in his awareness over a period of time. There is hardly enough information in his writings to speak emphatically about this. Still, we may note that instead of telling us how he sought this gift or resisted it or discovered it one day through some human agency such as prophecy (see I Tim. 4:14), he simply identifies it as his "own special gift *(charisma)* from God" (I Cor. 7:7). In this regard Paul does not consider himself exceptional, for he goes on to state that every believer has been granted such a personal charisma from God, "one of one kind and one of another" (I Cor. 7: 7b). This thought finds an echo in Rom., ch. 12, where Paul writes:

> By the grace given to me I bid every one among you not to think of himself more highly than he ought to think, but to think with sober judgment, each according to the measure of faith which God has assigned him. . . . Having gifts *(charismata)* that differ according to the grace given to us, let us use them. (Rom. 12:3ff.)

Ultimately, God alone distributes the charismata to believers according to his providential will. He does so, Paul notes, not to demonstrate his arbitrary might or to favor some individuals more highly than others, but to fashion communities of mutual care. Through bestowing his gifts according to his own plan and not simply according to our wishes, God always works to create a more harmonious and loving church.

Let us now return to the question we posed earlier. Is there one particular spiritual event or charisma which a believer must experience before becoming eligible for the higher gifts of prophecy, wisdom, knowledge, etc. (I Cor. 12:8–11)? The answer is no. We find so much variety in the New Testament data regarding the transmission of gifts that we must hesitate to make hard-and-fast rules. Sometimes the Spirit discloses itself in water baptism, sometimes prior to or afterward. Prayer and the laying on of hands may or may not precede the reception of higher charismata.[31] Spiritual gifts can be bestowed through a faithful response to the spoken (or read) word of the gospel. Christians defending their faith before the secular courts can count on a gift of bold speech from the Spirit, though they do not know ahead of time what form this will take. Believers may seek spiritual gifts through prayer and loving action, and, according to Luke, Jesus promises that God will never withhold the Spirit from those who ask (Luke 11:13). Yet the canonical authors carefully refrain from stating that the Spirit's advent will necessarily take the form of one or more of the charismata listed in I Cor., ch. 12. Finally, God alone determines the gift and the manner in which it is granted. Not once does the New Testament suggest that those who enjoy strong faith will thereby receive more or higher gifts, while those who suffer doubts or commit great sins will find themselves shortchanged. In this connection, we have only to consider Paul, the persecutor of the church![32]

To be sure, believers are urged to *do something* in order to receive spiritual gifts, that is, seek them. But no New Testament writer gives the slightest hint that any particular deed, "spiritual" experience, or charisma certifies a person for the reception of higher gifts. This kind of ladder-climbing runs counter to the gospel of justification by grace. To be sure, the New Testament does sometimes refer to a baptism in (or with) the Holy Spirit apart from water baptism (Matt. 3:11; Mark 1:8; Luke 3:16; John 1:33; Acts 1:5; 2:1–13; 11:15f.).[33] But there is no indication that this experi- ence should be regarded as normative or even frequent among believers, or that it functions as a necessary prelude to the reception of higher charismata. Paul never mentions it in his discussions of spiritual gifts. Instead, he presupposes that the Spirit who apportions charismata as it wills normally discloses itself to individuals for the first time as both giver and gift in water baptism (I Cor. 12: 11–13).[34]

Biblically considered, this is the sum of the matter. One need not be baptized in water to speak in tongues (Acts, ch. 10). One need not speak in tongues in order to receive the higher gifts of prophecy or, for that matter, any of the other charismata. One may speak in tongues or prophesy or practice other higher charismata, if God wills, without a baptism in the Holy Spirit distinct from water baptism (I Cor., ch. 14).[35]

There are only two common features in the numerous New Testament references to the granting of spiritual gifts. First, the individual recipient must be interested enough in God's gifts to want them, and to want them *from God*. This interest may manifest itself in the form of an obedient seeking (e.g., Cornelius in Acts, ch. 10) or a great need (the traumatized and blinded Paul in Damascus in Acts, ch. 9). To put it another way, there must be some consciousness in us, however minimal, of a God close at hand who is constantly trying to break through to us with his gifts. The seer John hears the risen Christ saying: "Behold, I stand at the door and knock; if any one hears my voice and opens the door, I will come in to him and eat with him, and he with me" (Rev. 3:20). Those who open, even if only a crack, are the people of God to whom the gifts of God will come.

A second common feature in the New Testament accounts of receiving gifts is that with one possible exception[36] gifts are *always* given in the presence of at least one other person, usually more. Paul's charisma of deliverance (from prison?) recorded in II Cor. 1:8–11 looks at first glance like a solitary gift, but it is not. Even if the "we" used throughout this passage does not include Paul's co-worker Timothy (and it probably does; see II Cor. 1:1), v. 11 shows that the apostle thought of those who prayed for his release as somehow "present," despite the fact that they were not physically there with him. We can render v. 11 literally as follows: "With you also helping in prayer on our behalf, in order that from many presences [or "faces"] the *charisma* granted to us through the agency of many [presences] might be acknowledged with thanksgiving on our behalf." In other words, Paul felt conscious of a great "cloud of witnesses" surrounding him (Heb. 12:1), a community of Christians in various locations appealing to God for his well-being and thanking God for his release. We find this communal aspect of gift reception confirmed in *every other* New Testament reference, if we allow that in Acts 9:17–19 Saul and Ananias constitute a congregation of two gathered in Jesus' name. Most often, gifts of the Spirit come to individuals within larger groups (e.g., Acts, ch. 2; 4:24ff.; 8:14ff.; 10:44ff.; 19:1ff.), and especially in the context of worship (Acts 13:1ff.; I Cor., chs. 12 to 14; probably Rom. 12:1ff. and I Peter 4:9–11). This is a powerful word about conditions for spiritual growth to Protestant North Americans (like the author) who tend to define religion as something one does in private.

One contemporary Christian group that seems to have caught the force of this New Testament directive is The Church of the Saviour in Washington, D.C. In her book *Eighth Day of Creation,* staff teacher Elizabeth O'Connor describes the group process in this church that enables it to become a "gift-evoking, gift-bearing community." Quoting minister Gordon Cosby, she writes:

> When each person is exercising his gift, he becomes an initiating center of life. . . . If there are ten people in one of the small groups of the church and each is an evoked person exercising his gift of the Spirit on behalf of the whole, then you have a group with power to attract. People gather around it. They respond to it, they love it, they hate it. Such a group has the power to heal, to liberate, to tackle the demonic systems and structures of society.[37]

As O'Connor goes on to demonstrate, one does not usually discover one's gift in isolation. Ordinarily, the community of believers mediates God's call to individuals by helping them identify those special gifts entrusted to them for the common good. Through the corporate body of believers one becomes "an evoked person."

O'Connor properly cautions her readers that receiving and exercising gifts in community may be no easy matter. It is a task that demands structure, discipline, struggle, trial and error. Negative feelings often intertwine with the joy of discovery. Inevitably, some believers envy the gifts of others; some despair of ever finding their gift; some, having recognized and claimed their gifts, experience disappointment because they are no longer searching, or they become fearful of the responsibility that accompanies the practice of their gifts on behalf of the community. Still others get stuck in their gifts, failing to recognize that God wants to draw them forward toward new challenges. Nevertheless, The Church of the Saviour has found that over the years its gift-evoking efforts repeatedly bear out the truth of Jesus' parable of the talents. The two servants in the story who trade with the talents entrusted to them thereby double their holdings. The master in the parable says: "Well done, good and faithful servant; you have been faithful over a little, I will set you over much; enter into the joy of your master" (Matt. 25: 23). This joy of the master, O'Connor writes, is what we receive for discerning and using God's gifts. It is a reward "not . . . in higher wages, another rung on the ladder, the acclaim of our peers, but in creative forces which flow within us and accomplish in our own lives the gracious work of transformation."[38] Those forces emerge most dramatically via the reception and initial practicing of spiritual gifts in a community of believers. Charismata pass freely through a group to individuals so that they can return to the group again as ministry.

Charismata and Charismatics: Working Definitions

Let us draw together what we have learned by fashioning tentative definitions of charismata and charismatics. If we have understood the New Testament witness correctly, the word *charisma,* used mostly by Paul, refers to a dazzling variety of gifts. They include the Spirit itself in some specific manifestation, changes in physical conditions and/or emotional states and dispositions, "ordinary" and "extraordinary" talents. Such gifts may be quite temporary, or they may last for a recipient's whole life. In every case the charisma is consciously received as a gift *from God.* Material objects as such are never named as charismata. The ability to raise or to give money might be a charisma, but money itself and the possession of it are not. God's special gifts always appear as energies or possibilities internalized by believers through divine grace; they come uniquely fitted to individuals. Though the New Testament identifies charismata as gifts of the Spirit (Rom. 1:11; I Cor. 12:1–11; 14:1), it prescribes no particular *experience* of the Spirit which must accompany them. Paul often speaks of charismata without mentioning the Spirit at all. Indeed, when he reflects upon the *origin* of charismata, his most common linguistic expression by far, whether stated or implied, is "the charisma of God" (Rom. 1: 8–12; 5:15f.; 6:23; 11:28, 29; 12:3–6; I Cor. 1:4–7; 7:7; 12:6, 27–31; II Cor. 1:8–11). No gift qualifies as a charisma unless the recipient sees behind it the gracious hand of God, for with the charisma one receives not simply a package, an objectified thing, but a new relationship with the Giver. One discovers afresh how one is dependent upon, in conversation with, answerable to, God. One learns in a richer way what it means to be a child of God (see II Cor. 1: 8–11).

This lesson shines through beautifully in a poem by the seventeenth-century English clergyman George Herbert. He entitles his work "The Collar." At the beginning of the poem the collar is a symbol for Herbert's priestly calling, which, after some years, he comes to experience as so frustrating and restrictive that he wants to tear it off, flee England, and "see the world":

> I struck the board, and cry'd, "No more,
>   I will abroad."
>   What, shall I ever sigh and pine?
> My lines and life are free; free as the road,
>   Loose as the wind, as large as store.
>   Shall I still be in suit?
>   Have I no harvest but a thorn
>   To let me blood, and not restore
>   What I have lost with cordial fruit?
>   Sure there was wine
> Before my sighs did dry it; there was corn
>   Before my tears did drown it;
>   Is the year only lost to me?
>   Have I no bays to crown it?
> No flowers, no garlands gay? all blasted,

All wasted?
Not so, my heart; but there is fruit,
   And thou hast hands.
Recover all thy sigh-blown age
On double pleasures; leave thy cold dispute
Of what is fit and not; forsake thy cage,
   Thy rope of sands
Which petty thoughts have made: and made to thee
   Good cable, to enforce and draw,
      And be thy law,
While thou didst wink and wouldst not see.
   Away: take heed:
   I will abroad.
Call in thy death's-head there, tie up thy fears.
   He that forbears
      To suit and serve his need
      Deserves his load.
But as I rav'd and grew more fierce and wild
   At every word,
Methought I heard one calling, "Child":
   And I replied, "My Lord."[39]

In the midst of his self-recrimination and rage to free himself from a prison of his own making, Herbert *thinks* he hears a word from God. And it is enough. In an instant that word recalls him to the true source of his vocation, thereby transforming his tight collar into a charisma.

We have seen a flexibility and open-endedness in Paul's use of the word *charisma* that could well have included Herbert's collar. The apostle applies the term to something as cosmic as "eternal life" (Rom. 6:23) and to something as historically bounded as his personal disposition toward celibacy (I Cor. 7:7) or his release from prison (II Cor. 1:8–11). We get the impression that Paul stands always on the edge of discovering new charismata and in no way intends his description of them in I Cor., ch. 12, and Rom., ch. 12, to be exhaustive. Yet the "higher" charismata, the *pneumatika,* do emerge as especially desirable. According to the apostle, these gifts, particularly prophecy, ought to be consciously sought after by believers. Again, the constant factor in this bewildering range of meanings is the believer's awareness at an identifiable moment that a particular gift has been crafted just for him or her by the hand of God.

Charismata characteristically lead their recipients into ministry, even if the call to service is not sensed immediately at the time the gifts are bestowed. Sometimes God discloses himself to us in charismata chiefly to restore and refresh us. Later, when we have gained strength, we learn how to use our gifts. By contrast, other charismata are given in the thick of ministry; we know right away which callings they will help us to answer.

To summarize, we may think of a charisma as a supremely divine-personal gift. It is, on the one hand, uniquely "ours" and could be no one else's. It carries with it the power to shape both our individual and corporate identities as believers. On the other hand, a charisma is not really ours at all, for its reception has the effect of teaching us that nothing belongs to us by right or achievement; all is a trust from the One greater than ourselves. At the very moment when we confess, "All things are ours" (I Cor. 3:21f.), we also acknowledge, with thanksgiving, that we ourselves belong to Christ and through Christ to God (v. 23). In short, charismata are the gifts of God for the people of God.

Who, then, should be called "charismatics"? Since this word never occurs in the Bible, our answer must be speculative. However, it seems legitimate to conclude from the New Testament data that if Paul or Luke *had* used the word, they would have meant by it simply those people who respond with awe and humility to a gift suddenly perceived. Charismatics would be people who see the Giver behind the gift and utter the words, "My Lord."

CHAPTER 5

The Gift of the Cross

Individuals who perceive God's presence in their gifts frequently experience a vigorous joy. Often their attitudes and behavior patterns are so transformed that they begin to think of themselves as altogether new people. Some fifteen years ago John Sherrill, a Christian magazine writer, underwent what he came to call a baptism in the Holy Spirit. He describes the three months immediately following this event as "one long smile":

> Never had I known such a protracted period of well-being. . . .
>
> Many deep-rooted psychological quirks, which I had used most of my life to keep people at a safe distance, disappeared entirely during these months. I got to know old friends on an entirely different level and made new ones without the shyness which is my usual lot.
>
> Bible reading moved into a new direction. . . . It was a phenomenal adventure, reading words I'd focused my eyes upon all my life yet never grasped. For the first time I approached the Gospels and Acts as descriptive rather than poetry reading. I read stories of miracles, demons, healings, spirits with brand new eyes. . . .
>
> I used my new tongue, too, during this period. There were two kinds of occasions when it seemed to come naturally. One was in response to beauty. I remember one January morning in particular when every twig on every tree was coated with ice. I looked out the bedroom window at this glittering world and it seemed the most natural thing in the world to express the indescribable in sound alone. . . .
>
> The other times when I used [tongues] were in intercessions. I

remember praying in tongues one evening for a man in our parish whose wife had confided to us that her husband wasn't sleeping nights. That was all she said and since I scarcely knew the man it was useless to try to offer intelligent prayer for him.

At three o'clock that morning I woke up, stark awake, with the conviction that the man's problem was a long-standing resentment of one of the people where he worked, that he had never forgiven this other person for this ancient injury, and furthermore that I had to go and face him with the idea. I could not get back to sleep until I resolved to do it.[1]

Sherrill goes on to narrate how he timidly confronted the man, Bill, with his "hunch" and found it to be precisely correct. Bill was dumbfounded, but as a result of this exposure he soon found himself freed from his burden.[2] Clearly, Sherrill discovered in his charisma both a renewed identity and a healing mission within the body of Christ—just what we would expect from our study of the New Testament.

The fact that Sherrill's reception of the Spirit resembled a conversion experience makes his extravagant language understandable. His life really had begun to take on an extraordinarily different hue. Paul too was a seasoned charismatic who presumably had enjoyed gifts of the Spirit for years prior to his correspondence with the Corinthians (I Cor. 14:19; II Cor. 12:11–13; Rom. 15:18f.). Yet he reports a dramatic change in his life following the charisma of his release from prison (II Cor. 1:8–11). It was a new turning from self-reliance (a besetting sin, even for apostles!) to trust in God. It seemed, Paul writes, as if he had died and been raised again by God —so radical was the event (II Cor. 1:9). It may have been precisely then that the apostle let go of his "conviction" that he would live to welcome Christ back to earth (I Thess. 4:17; I Cor. 15:51f.) and began to reflect on the possibility of his death prior to the Second Coming (II Cor. 5:2–8; Phil. 1:20ff.). We cannot know for sure. The point is that even this very gifted man in Christ found he could be *further* transformed by a new charisma. Out of his release came a fresh confidence and zeal for ministry (Phil. 1:10f.). This sense of fullness seems to be the typical initial response of believers to the discovery of a charisma. But, just as typically, the fullness does not last.

Giftedness and Groaning

After his three-month "smile" Sherrill began to suspect that his whole charismatic experience was nothing more than a self-generated illusion. Tongues no longer came so easily. When they did, he feared that he, not the Holy Spirit, was inducing them. Along with these doubts lurked the suggestion that his newfound wholeness had been achieved quite naturally and could therefore be maintained without further dependence upon God. Sherrill describes this turnabout as "violent," though relatively short-lived.[3]

The New Testament does not tell us comparable stories about the trials befalling rejuvenated believers (although Jesus' temptation in the desert at the hand of Satan is sometimes cited as a parallel). Its authors, however, do recognize that with the charismata come negative experiences as well as pleasurable ones. Again, it is Paul who wrestles most courageously with this phenomenon. In Rom. 12:3–6 he warns his readers that they must consider their charismata to be limitations as well as powers. To receive one gift means that one does not receive another. Jealousy remains a perpetual danger. Thus Paul writes:

> By the grace given to me I bid every one among you not to think of himself more highly than he ought to think, but to think with sober judgment, each according to the measure of faith which God has assigned him. For as in one body we have many members, and all the members do not have the same function, so we, though many, are one body in Christ, and individually members one of another. Having gifts (charismata) that differ according to the grace given to us, let us use them. (Rom. 12:3–6)

Paul counsels the Romans that they should strive to practice more faithfully the charismata they already have. Simultaneously, they must resist the temptation to exalt themselves above their neighbors by trying to leap beyond their gifts. Here the charismata act

as a fence around pride; they place a check on the believer's potentially arrogant self-image. We can guess that at least some of Paul's
Roman readers found this news disappointing.

But limitation is not the only dis-ease received along with the
charismata. More poignant perhaps is the deep sense of longing for
full redemption introduced by the Spirit. Paul writes of this in two
places, both having to do with the relationship between God's
Spirit and the physical order. In II Cor., ch. 5, he says:

> We know that if the earthly tent we live in [the body] is destroyed,
> we have a building from God, a house not made with hands, eternal
> in the heavens. Here indeed we groan, and long to put on our
> heavenly dwelling, so that by putting it on we may not be found
> naked. For while we are still in this tent, we sigh with anxiety; not
> that we would be unclothed, but that we would be further clothed,
> so that what is mortal may be swallowed up by life. He who has
> prepared us for this very thing is God, who has given us the Spirit
> as a guarantee. (II Cor. 5:1–5)

Here the believer's life appears anything but tranquil. On the contrary, it exhibits anxiety and yearning for a better condition. The
Spirit "guarantees" that a future homecoming will take place, but
at the same time its pledge creates dissatisfaction with one's present
state. In Rom., ch. 8, Paul reflects on the cosmic dimension of the
believer's longing:

> We know that the whole creation has been groaning in travail
> together until now; and not only the creation, but we ourselves,
> who have the first fruits of the Spirit, groan inwardly as we
> wait for adoption as sons, the redemption of our bodies. (Rom.
> 8:22f.)

It would be wrong to interpret this passage as a joyful celebration
of birth pangs. Paul is talking about pain and a sense of incomplete-
ness (see also Rom. 8:24ff.). He finds it ironic that God's Spirit, the
firstfruits of salvation and harbinger of the age to some, binds
believers more closely than ever before to the sufferings of the
present material order (Rom. 8:18–21). Charismata make us sensitive to afflictions we have never been aware of; they point us to the

anguished "not-yet" of God's redemptive work. And that is not easy to take.

Paul goes still farther:

> Likewise the Spirit helps us in our weakness; for we do not know how to pray as we ought, but the Spirit himself intercedes for us with sighs too deep for words [literally: "with wordless groanings"]. (Rom. 8:26)

Ernst Käsemann has shown that in this striking passage Paul focuses on none other than glossolalia, the charisma of tongues.[4] The surprising point of Paul's statement is that tongues, the language of angels (I Cor. 13:1), may serve as a profound expression not only of fullness but also of deficiency, weakness, and emptiness. Käsemann argues that in this context we would be true to Paul if we called tongues a "cry for liberty."[5] According to the apostle, believers speak in tongues not least in order to ask for help.[6] Their charisma bespeaks both the Spirit's aid and their own yawning human need. The implications of this are shattering for believers who consistently desire to think of themselves as powerful by virtue of their charismata. Paul implies that it is precisely the charismatics who can face their own weakness most realistically.[7] Gifted as they are, they must acknowledge that they do not even know how to pray. In the sighing of their tongues the Spirit prays for them.

As a final example of the groaning inaugurated by the Spirit and its gifts let us examine the well-known fifth chapter of Galatians. Here Paul contrasts "the desires of the flesh" with the "desires of the Spirit" (Gal. 5:16ff.). The former lead not only to immoderate bodily appetites but also to such negative inclinations of the human spirit as "idolatry, sorcery, enmity, strife, jealousy, anger, selfishness, dissension, party spirit, [and] envy" (Gal. 5:20f.). The latter yield what Paul calls "the fruit of the Spirit," i.e., "love, joy, peace, patience, kindness, goodness, faithfulness, gentleness, [and] self-control" (Gal. 5:22f.). True to form, Paul discerns a paradox in all of this. The quiet virtues which he enumerates seem to blossom forth only as the by-product of a fierce struggle within the believer. The Spirit does not just take over a believer's inner life, immediately banishing his or her "fleshly" lusts. Instead, its advent awakens and challenges these urges, thus touching off a lively battle. "For the desires of the flesh are against the Spirit, and the desires of the Spirit are against the flesh; for these are opposed to each other, to prevent you from doing what you [according to the fleshly inclination] would." (Gal. 5:17.) Paul does not spell it out in so many words, but his meaning is surely that God purposely initiates this conflict through the gift of his Spirit. In the Spirit he swats the sleeping dragon of the flesh on its nose; he invades its heretofore "peaceful" domain. In other words, the spiritual love, joy, and peace that Paul has in mind are not in any simple way to be identified with good feelings, for they coexist with the considerable anxiety of a more or less constant inner war. We have alluded to the Spirit's role as warrior in Chapter 3. Here we want to point up the Pauline observation that its presence may heighten, not alleviate, moral conflict. In this way too, charismata sometimes increase the believer's groaning.

Special Gifts, Special Wounds

The Biblical record reveals yet another sober fact. On occasion, unusually gifted individuals are "presented" with severe and lasting burdens. Indeed, these vexations may come interwoven with a particular gift, like the warp of a fabric with its woof. The Old Testament story of Jacob's combat with the angel (Gen. 32:22–32) illustrates this mysterious facet of God's providence. As the story goes, Jacob's opponent (the angel of the Lord?) recognizes at the very outset of their struggle that he cannot defeat this determined mortal, so he disables Jacob early on by putting his thigh out of joint. The pain does not stop Jacob, who clings to the angel for all he is worth. In the end he wrests a blessing from the stranger, who tells him, " 'Your name shall no more be called Jacob, but Israel, for you have striven with God and with men, and have prevailed.' . . . And there he blessed him" (Gen. 32:28f.). Jacob's blessing lasts. His name becomes the self-designation for God's chosen people, and his sons father its twelve tribes. But Jacob's wound also lasts. "The sun rose upon him as he passed Penuel, limping because of his thigh." (Gen. 32:31.) Both are the gifts of God, the pain as well as the horizon bright with blessing.

In the New Testament we encounter two paradigmatic servants of God whose gifts intertwine with their wounds. We speak of Jesus and Paul. It may seem inappropriate to compare Jesus' gifts with those of others; in so many respects the New Testament writers consider him to be absolutely unique. Nevertheless, the Evangelists insist that believers must imitate Jesus by taking up their cross (Mark 8:34; Matt. 16:24; Luke 9:23). For this reason alone we do well to ponder the fact that according to all four Gospels Jesus understands his impending suffering and death as a "cup" offered to him by his Father (Mark 14:36; Matt. 26:39; Luke 22:42; John 18:11). John states it most explicitly. In his account of the betrayal in Gethsemane we find this saying of Jesus to Peter: "Put your sword into its sheath; shall I not drink the cup which the Father has given me?" The Bible does not shrink from crediting God with such heavy "gifts."

Paul's case is somewhat more subtle but in the end makes this same point. On the one hand, the apostle rejoices in his calling as a gift of grace which has enabled him to work harder than any of his missionary colleagues (I Cor. 15:10f.) On the other hand, he also sees that his gift for ministry has brought with it great sufferings—imprisonments, beatings, and deprivations of food and shelter (II Cor. 11:23–27)—plus "the daily pressure upon me of my anxiety for all the churches" (v. 28). Thus far, Paul leaves the connection between his calling and his apostolic sufferings implicit; he never says that God *gave* him these afflictions. But at one point he does dare to claim exactly that. It happens in II Cor. 12:1–10 where he recounts the origin of his "thorn in the flesh," probably a somatic illness or injury.[8] The painful gift is preceded by a glorious one: a visionary trip to the third heaven where Paul "heard things that cannot be told, which man cannot utter" (II Cor. 12: 4). But as soon as he returns to everyday life in the body Paul makes a mortifying discovery:

> To keep me from being too elated by the abundance of revelations, a thorn was given me in the flesh, a messenger of Satan, to harass

me, to keep me from being too elated. Three times I besought the
Lord about this, that it should leave me; but he said to me, "My
grace is sufficient for you, for my power is made perfect in weakness." (II Cor. 12:7–9)

Does Paul really mean to say that this messenger of Satan is a gift
from God? It appears so. The apostle, who surely knew the story
of Job, would have seen no contradiction between Satan's agency
and God's permission (Job 1:6ff.). But Paul goes beyond the Old
Testament story. Job was a righteous man whose trials represented
a test of loyalty to God induced by a skeptical Satan. Paul suggests
that in his own case it was none other than God who had actively
initiated the fixing of his thorn to keep him from becoming too
proud. It was a preventative "gift" from on high. Satan's interest
would have been to encourage Paul's pride. Following his prayers
that the thorn might be removed, Paul learns from the risen Lord
that his vexation will remain to serve a second purpose: through
his weakness the power of Christ will be "made perfect" (II Cor.
12:9), that is, it will blossom into full view. As far as we know,
Paul's thorn never left him.

Here we confront an odd and even frightening teaching. At
times, a pain or an illness—in Paul's case an abiding one—may be
God's gift to us. It may become a grace-filled opportunity for us
to receive and display God's power. The Dutch priest-psychologist
Henri Nouwen writes of this paradox in his book, *The Wounded
Healer.* He focuses especially upon the psychic pain of loneliness
common to all who embark upon ministry:

> We see how loneliness is the [lay as well as clerical] minister's
> wound not only because he shares in the human condition, but also
> because of the unique predicament of his profession. It is this wound
> which he is called to bind with more care and attention than others
> usually do. For a deep understanding of his own pain makes it
> possible for him to convert his weakness into strength and to offer
> his own experience as a source of healing to those who are often lost
> in the darkness of their own misunderstood sufferings.[9]

Nouwen seems to be saying that since loneliness becomes the inevi-
table companion of anyone who wants to take ministry seriously,

it will somehow (if God is gracious) turn out to be a resource for ministry. Paul would surely have agreed. On the other hand, good Jew that he was, he would also have warned us not to accept our pains too courteously. When he first perceived his thorn, he was hardly willing to understand it as a gift from God. Instead, he protested vigorously to the Lord in three seasons of prayer (II Cor. 12:8), arguing, we may suspect, that this thorn scarcely befitted God's chosen apostle to the Gentiles. Wounded healers were not popular in the first century, especially in Jewish circles where religious leaders like the high priest had to be without physical spot or blemish. According to the conventional wisdom of the day, apostles had to make a good appearance if they expected to attract people to their message. (See II Cor. 10:9f.) In time, Paul learned that his thorn was a gift. But his resistance to that interpretation also remains part of the canonical record. Perhaps God wants to alert us through it to the danger of masochism. Healing is always a possibility; not all thorns are "given" to last.

Paul refrains from calling his thorn a charisma. But he might have done so, for it meets all the criteria we have discerned for identifying such a gift. For example, the thorn is a feature of Paul's believing existence, uniquely fitted to his own body. It is (finally) acknowledged by him as a channel for God's grace in his ministry. He learns something about the nature of God from it and, at the end, even expresses thanksgiving for it:

> I will all the more gladly boast in my weaknesses, that the power of Christ may rest upon me. For the sake of Christ, then, I am content with weaknesses, insults, hardships, persecutions, and calamities; for when I am weak, then I am strong. (II Cor. 12:9f.)

Above all, Paul comes to see that through this affliction God draws near to him, and, through him, to others (see II Cor. 4:7–12). In this respect Paul's thorn looks much like George Herbert's collar. It is a calling that cramps, but for all its pain it is a divine calling.

Receiving Christ's Passion

"For it has been granted [*echaristhē* means "bestowed as a gracious gift"] to you for the sake of Christ [that] you should not only believe in him but also suffer for his sake, engaged in the same conflict which you saw and now hear to be mine" (Phil. 1:29f.). So Paul addresses the Philippians. The suffering he has in mind may be some specific persecution—he is, after all, writing from prison (Phil. 1:7, 13, 17), and in v. 28 he refers to the Philippians' "opponents." But the word he uses for "conflict" does not usually denote so much an *oppression* by exterior forces as a "contest" or "struggle." Our best commentary on the suffering for Christ which the Philippians have received as a gift is found in v. 27:

> Only let your manner of life be worthy of the gospel of Christ, so that whether I come and see you or am absent, I may hear of you that you stand firm in one spirit, with one mind striving side by side for the faith of the gospel. (Phil. 1:27)

In v. 29, then, suffering for Christ's sake probably means standing up for one's faith through one's life-style, whatever the consequences. Such suffering does not mean simply opposition or persecution from the outside (though these may occur); it also means overcoming inertia and fear from within. In Paul's mind suffering for Christ's sake would include a believer's effort to live in love, harmony, and humility with others (Phil. 2:1–5). It would be much the same thing as working out one's own salvation "with fear and trembling" (Phil. 2:12).

The point is not to argue that sharing Christ's sufferings has nothing to do with persecution. Paul states most emphatically that his apostolic adversities, which include persecution, result from "the death of Jesus" which he bears in his body during the course of his ministry (II Cor. 4:7–12; see also I Cor. 4:9–13; II Cor. 6: 3–10; 11:23–33; Col. 1:24). What the Philippians passage adds to this interpretation is that the "gift" of suffering for Christ's sake may also mean something other than harassment by civil and religious authorities, or even by friends. It may refer to inner conflict. The Gospels seem to allow for such a psychological definition of sharing Christ's suffering when they record these words of Jesus:

> If any man would come after me, let him deny himself and take up his cross and follow me. For whoever would save his life will lose it; and whoever loses his life for my sake and the gospel's will save it. (Mark 8:34; Matt. 16:24)

Matthew and Mark undoubtedly understand Jesus' admonition as a message to those who must face martyrdom (see Mark 10:35–39). But it is highly questionable, in the light of the broad readership they wish to address, whether these Evangelists intend to limit the cross to physical death. Luke, at any rate, makes it clear that he does not. His version of the saying reads, "If any man would come after me, let him deny himself and take up his cross *daily* and follow me" (Luke 9:23, italics added). Probably all three Gospel writers want to allow their readers the possibility of understanding the word "cross" metaphorically as the constant struggle to live a life of discipleship to Jesus. But again, it is Paul who sees most clearly that this struggle may be experienced as a gift.

New Testament writers often place the sharing of Christ's sufferings in the context of cosmic upheavals initiated by the resurrection. When Paul says that we are "heirs of God and fellow heirs with Christ, provided we suffer with him" (Rom. 8:17), he is probably thinking about the so-called "woes of the Messiah" which were expected by many Jews to accompany the Anointed One's advent.[10] The idea was that God's Messiah could only establish his reign on earth after he had first defeated all opposing powers, both human and satanic. (See Matt., ch. 24; Mark, ch. 13; Luke, ch. 21; Rev., chs. 19 to 21.) Paul understands Jesus' resurrection as the beginning of this cosmic battle. For him, the risen Christ is no sedentary monarch resting from the labors of his earthly ministry. Rather, he is an active general constantly leading his people against "every rule and every authority and power" that still contests his reign (I Cor. 15:24ff.). By virtue of their incorporation into the church all believers receive a share in Christ's militant suffering for the world (see Acts 9:1–5). They are baptized into his continuing death (II Cor. 4:10f.; Phil. 3:10) so that they can strive against the tenaciously powerful dominion of sin (Rom. 6:1–14). To put it another way, the gift of the Spirit, ordinarily received in baptism, becomes a call to arms against satanic forces.

Believers generally encounter these superhuman powers in the form of temptations—literally, "tests" in the Greek (I Thess. 3:5; Gal. 6:1; I Cor. 7:5; 10:1–13). This is a common idea in Judaism as well as in many other religions. But Paul does not appear to be thinking of the normal temptations suffered by God's faithful people in all ages. Instead, he perceives that the "fulness of the time" in which he and his readers live (Gal. 4:4) will be the last period in world history. He senses that even as he writes, "the form of this world is passing away" (I Cor. 7:31). This means that believers are witnessing the final showdown between good and evil, a heightening of their ancient conflict at every level of creation. Consequently, the temptations they suffer will become terribly severe; upon them "the end of the ages has come" (I Cor. 10:11f.). If we want to remain true to the New Testament, we dare not reduce these temptations to the believing individual's personal struggle against his or her negative character traits. As the writer to the Ephesians puts it:

> We are not contending against flesh and blood, but against the principalities, against the powers, against the world rulers of this present darkness, against the spiritual hosts of wickedness in the heavenly places. (Eph. 6:12)

In their death gasp the hellish powers will wreak immense destruction—especially upon Christ's followers (Matt. 24:9–12; Rev. 12: 13 to 13:7; 17:6). Although they cannot finally prevail, the satanic forces will torment believers with every imaginable "tribulation, or distress, or persecution, or famine, or nakedness, or peril, or sword" (Rom. 8:35 read in the light of vs. 36–38). These are the messianic woes, "the sufferings of this present time" which believers begin to share with Christ as soon as they have received the Spirit (Rom. 8:14–18).

How can we reconcile such a view with what we have discovered about the earliest believers' extraordinary sense of giftedness (Chapter 2)? Paul would see no difficulty. He would tell us that in "this age," infested as it is with evil, the true joy of receiving God's charismata will always provoke Satan's wrath. Every new charisma, greeted with human thanksgiving to God, diminishes Satan's power, and Satan will not take that passively. Paul would probably even want to say that unless we eventually experience some definable vulnerability to the principalities and powers, we have no right to speak of our gifts as charismata. In some mysterious way God's Spirit comes mixed through and through with the cosmic sufferings of Christ. Every charisma therefore carries with it the gift of the cross.

> When we cry, "Abba! Father!" it is the Spirit himself bearing witness with our spirit that we are children of God, and if children, then heirs, heirs of God and fellow heirs with Christ, provided we suffer with him. (Rom. 8:15–17)

Two angles in the discussion above may prove unusually troublesome. First, can we possibly agree with Paul that we are living in the world's last days? Since the end did not come as he expected it to, is there any reason now, nineteen centuries later, to live as if it were just around the corner? Don't the odd Christian sects who set dates for Christ's return do more harm than good by raising false expectations? Though we cannot respond fully to these legitimate questions, we can say this much. Even though Paul was wrong about the *temporal* nearness of the world's consummation, he may have been right about the "fulness of time." That is, it would still be possible to argue that the resurrection has changed the quality of world history by initiating a prolonged heightening in the conflict between good and evil. This is not the same as claiming that Christ and the church have made our world a better place to live in. The New Testament never says this, and it must certainly be regarded as a questionable hypothesis today in the light of what we know about church history. Nor is the heightening we refer to an indirect boast that confessed Christians, in contrast to others, stand most often on the side of good. All we are saying in Paul's defense is that he may have seen clearly into the meaning of the resurrection: it was not the end but the beginning of God's final war against Satan's forces.

This very assertion may well raise a second major objection. How can we twentieth-century believers respond to the New Testament's preoccupation with superhuman powers of evil? Is there really a personal Satan? Aren't people just dodging responsibility when they say "the devil made me do it"? Don't those who participate in contemporary charismatic movements rush to perform exorcisms when they should be referring people to psychotherapists? Again, we lack the space (not to mention the wisdom) to give these questions the answers they deserve. But one important point needs to be made: it is getting much harder these days to explain human behavior, whether individual or corporate, in terms of secular psychological and sociological theories. The more we learn about humanity, the more mysteries we encounter. Were the moral stupor of Hitler's Third Reich and the heinous holocaust it produced really predictable? Were they solely the result of human action and inaction? Christian readers must decide for themselves how to fit such monumental evil together with their conviction that God's love extends indiscriminately to all people.[11]

There is at least one other way in which the New Testament reflects upon sharing Christ's suffering (and death) as a charismatic gift. At the risk of trivializing it, we might call this appropriation of Christ's passion "growing pains." Paul hints at it in Phil., ch. 3, when he writes that even as a believer he must press onward "that I may know him [Christ] and the power of his resurrecton, and may share his sufferings, becoming like him in his death, that if possible I may attain the resurrection from the dead" (Phil. 3: 10f.). In traditional theological terms, Paul is talking about the foundations for sanctification. In his opinion, it is a mark of Christian maturity (see Phil. 3:15) to be constantly on the move, always aware that one has not yet been perfected in grace, always "forgetting what lies behind and straining forward to what lies ahead" (vs. 12–13). We ought to notice that what Paul eagerly anticipates is, in part, an expanded share in Christ's suffering and death. He takes this unusual position because he strongly believes that through such experiences will come deeper dimensions of resurrection power, especially power for ministry (see II Cor. 1:3–7; 4:7–12; 12: 9–10; 13:4).

Paul holds the view that all believers ought to be undergoing a constant transformation, a renewal of their minds which enables them to discern God's will more clearly and enact it more forcefully (Rom. 12:1–2). But this transformation/renewal is a painful process. It often requires the sacrifice of one's dearest opinions and practices—sometimes even those which one has acquired as a believer. Paul probably has such a transformation in mind when he says that he dies every day (I Cor. 15:31) and when he describes his life as an "affliction" through which "our outer nature is wasting away [while] our inner nature is being renewed every day" (II Cor. 4:16f.). The apostle has noted, just a few verses earlier, that he carries "the death of Jesus" in his body and is therefore "always being given up to death for Jesus' sake" (II Cor. 4:10f.). We may suspect that he sees a causal connection between this continual dying and the renewal process (see also Rom. 6:6), especially when we notice that the dying he refers to in II Cor. 4:8–10 includes psychological dimensions like perplexity as well as bodily persecutions.

Can this participation in Christ's suffering and death for renewal really be called a gift? That is what Paul seems to be saying in II Cor. 1:8–11 when he describes his deliverance in Asia as a charisma (v. 11, translated "blessing" in the RSV). Previously we have cited this passage as evidence that Paul understood his release from prison to be a special gift of God's grace. But the text may require a broader interpretation. Let us examine it once again:

> For we do not want you to be ignorant, brethren, of the affliction we experienced in Asia; for we were so utterly, unbearably crushed that we despaired of life itself. Why, we felt that we had received the sentence of death; but that was to make us rely not on ourselves but on God who raises the dead. (II Cor. 1:8–9)

It looks as if Paul, in retrospect, has moved toward the conclusion that even his despair was intended by God for his good. Part of him had to die before his faith could be raised to a higher degree of resiliency. If this view is correct, then the label that Paul attaches to his story, charisma, must include the death part of his experience as well as the resurrection/liberation part. The entire event was a blessing: God gave him an enlarged share in Christ's dying (see II Cor. 1:5–7) so that through it he could receive newness of life.

Joy in the Gift of the Cross

Joy is a complex human experience. It must be more than happiness, for while it seems excluded by such psychological states as despair, it can nevertheless coexist with other types of mental and physical suffering. Perhaps that is because true joy looks beyond the immediate moment into a wider reality. In his autobiography, *Surprised by Joy,* C. S. Lewis tells how from early childhood he was overtaken, periodically, by powerful visions of mystical grandeur and wholeness. Since these moments proved most satisfying, he found, as he grew, that he was trying hard to induce them, usually without success. When he became a Christian, Lewis discovered that the "joy" which he was seeking so passionately needed to be reinterpreted. His own words tell the story best.

> I now know that the experience, considered as a state of my own mind, had never had the kind of importance I once gave it. It was valuable only as a pointer to something other and outer. While that other was in doubt, the pointer naturally loomed large in my thoughts. When we are lost in the woods the sight of a signpost is a great matter. He who first sees it cries, "Look!" The whole party gathers round and stares. But when we have found the road and are passing signposts every few miles, we shall not stop and stare. They will encourage us and we shall be grateful to the authority that set them up. But we shall not stop and stare, or not much; not on this road, though their pillars are of silver and their lettering of gold. "We would be at Jerusalem."[12]

Joy keeps its eyes fixed on "the Jerusalem above" (Gal. 4:26; Rev., ch. 21). Thus it can tolerate and transform earthly pain. Paul says believers are to rejoice in suffering because the Holy Spirit within them, God's pledge of love, will use these trials to produce endurance, character, and, above all, hope for the future (Rom. 5:3–5;

see also James 1:2). Such joy becomes easier to sense when believers know that they are sharing Christ's sufferings through persecution (I Peter 4:12–13). To some readers this may sound almost pathological. Yet we are not dealing here with a *desire* for suffering. According to the New Testament writers, joy can surface in the midst of and in spite of suffering, but it cannot be identified with the latter. As we learned in Chapter 2, joy forms the melody line of a believer's life. Sometimes we feel it; sometimes we must remember it and proclaim its reality even when we do not feel it. But like the Lord himself, it always stands close "at hand" (Phil. 4:4f.).

Paul's mature thoughts on the interpenetration of joy and suffering emerge most clearly in the exquisite little essay we call the letter to the Philippians.[13] The apostle writes this letter—or part of it, at least—from prison (Phil. 1:7, 13, 19). He reckons with the possibility of his death in the near future (Phil. 1:19–26), acknowledges the suffering of the Philippians (vs. 28–30), enjoins them to work out their salvation with fear and trembling (Phil. 2:12), and urges them to imitate him in sharing Christ's sufferings (Phil. 3:7–17). Nevertheless, the language of joy abounds. In fact, the various forms of *chara* ("joy") and *chairō* ("rejoicing") occur more frequently per page here than in any other New Testament document (see Phil. 1:4, 25; 2:2, 17, 18, 28, 29; 3:1; 4:1, 10). With almost every new thought Paul pauses either to blurt out his own joy or to encourage the Philippians in theirs. Why? The fact that Paul expects to be released from prison soon (Phil. 1:25f.; 2:24) must play a role. He is obviously in a buoyant, affectionate mood (e.g., Phil. 1:19–26; 4: 1, 9). But there seems to be more to it than that. In his own mind at least Paul thinks he has found out something new about the "peace of God, which passes all understanding" (Phil. 4:7). He might even be referring to the charisma of release narrated in II Cor. 1:8–11. At any rate, near the end of his letter he offers his readers a resolution in his life that has been long in coming:

> I have learned, in whatever state I am, to be content. I know how to be abased, and I know how to abound; in any and all circumstances I have learned the secret [literally: I have been initiated into

the mystery] of facing plenty and hunger, abundance and want. I can do all things in him who strengthens me. (Phil. 4:11–13)

There is a quietness about this confession not quite characteristic of the volatile Paul. Now, after years of apostleship, he *knows* that Christ reigns over all occasions. Therefore all is a gift. Therefore he must rejoice.

Our purpose in this chapter has been to contemplate the dark side of God's charismata. Often, perhaps always, they carry with them a consciously felt new immersion into Christ's sufferings. From a bodily or psychic point of view, this is at least unpleasant, at most terrifying. To be a charismatic in the New Testament sense, one need not, indeed cannot be constantly happy.

On the other hand, precisely because the crucified Christ rules as Lord, every limitation, struggle, and pain becomes a potential messenger from God. Each door slammed in our faces may be his invitation to turn around and discover other doors we never saw before. Often a charisma comes as both binding and new freedom. Only those who are willing to undergo such renewals frequently—Paul calls them daily death (I Cor. 15:31)—can live for long the charismatic life. Amazingly, there is joy in all this: a steady, durable joy as different from our culturally produced emotional highs as plastic from fine oak.

CHAPTER 6

From Gift
to Task
to Giver

Interplay abounds among charismata, the works of ministry to which they lead, and God, the source of every good and perfect gift.[1] The chapter title will prove misleading if we imagine that the motion it describes is unidirectional along a straight line or in a circle. The whole matter proves immensely more complex than that—and fortunately so. It would be hard indeed if we thought we had to move, lockstep, from gift to task to Giver in our consciousness. This would constitute a pattern that perhaps conforms to some of our experience, but by no means all of it. We would be doing ourselves (and the New Testament) an injustice if we tried to force our Christian life into such a narrow mold. The chapter title suggests a reciprocity of motion among gift, task, and Giver. It is not the boringly predictable back and forth of a piston engine, but the flowing symmetry of a corps de ballet or the spontaneous give and go of a well-coached basketball team. A diagram (on p. 147) may help to make this point clearer and also set our agenda for the rest of the chapter.

As believers, we find ourselves somewhere along the broken line in our sensitivity to gift, task, and Giver.[2] If we stand at the far left, we feel gifted and close to God. He wills, however, to push us off this comfortable mountaintop toward our proper tasks in the world. Some believers respond well, moving rapidly from left to right and back again. Others trudge slowly and with great reluctance. It is a mark of Christian growth to make that daily commutation more easily.

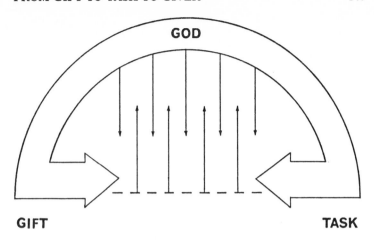

If we presently stand at the far right, we probably sense a great weight of responsibility for a particular task at hand. We assent to its goodness; we know that the job before us is of God and needs to be done *by us.* Perhaps we are even aware of God's shoving. But we do not feel gifted enough to accomplish the work. At such moments God wants to move our consciousness in the direction of his gifts so that we can act. As we have noted in Chapter 4, commenting on II Cor. 9:6–11, the consciousness that sets us in motion may be that of faith in God's liberal giving, not the actual reception of charismata, which comes later.

If we get stuck somewhere along the middle of the broken line, we are probably oblivious to either divine gift or divine task, and God himself may seem far away. But the vertical up-and-down arrows symbolize the New Testament writers' conviction that not even this human situation is without access to God. We can speak with him, and he with us, wherever we are. If we feel giftless or taskless and without purpose, we can tell him so. Paul was not above complaining, for that too was an act of faith as he understood it (II Cor. 12:8). If the New Testament tells us the truth about God, he may well answer us by reminding us of some gifts and tasks we have forgotten; or he may reveal new ones.

To readers who are suffering from a long absence of God's

discernible power in their lives, what we have just said may seem hopelessly simplistic, even flippant. It is not so intended. Anyone who has suffered or worked in a hospital will know how soon our puny human systems for understanding God's plans break down, even when they claim to be Biblical. Paul knew this too (I Cor. 15: 31; II Cor. 1:8–11; Rom., ch. 11). We are all in kindergarten at God's school. Even the most spiritual can do no more than glimpse his ways "in a mirror dimly" (I Cor. 13:12). What we have sketched above therefore must be considered an attempt to organize the New Testament data for the sake of communication and future learning. It is an experiment: a hypothesis to be tested by the texts and by our lives, not the answer to all our questions. Properly done, exegesis always leads to further mysteries. On that note of realism let us proceed.

Walk in Love, by the Spirit

One hesitates to say anything more about the New Testament understanding of love *(agapē)*. So much has already been written. Despite the huge quantity of reliable information available to us, we have managed to confuse what the word signifies with feelings of romance, general amiability, or moderate philanthropy. This is not the place to set about correcting such monumental misunderstandings. Yet we must speak about love, for we find that three out of the four New Testament gift lists (I Cor., chs. 12 to 14; Eph. 4: 7–16; I Peter 4:7–11) come linked with pointed references to *agapē*.[3] The juxtaposition suggests that love has some vital role to play in the movements to and fro among gifts, task, and Giver. Let us see if we can determine whether this view holds true and, if so, what love's role is. The passage in I Peter goes as follows:

> The end of all things is at hand; therefore keep sane and sober for your prayers. Above all hold unfailing your love for one another, since love covers a multitude of sins. Practice hospitality ungrudgingly to one another. As each has received a gift *(charisma)*, employ it for one another [literally: "serve it up to one another as a waiter"], as good stewards of God's varied grace. (I Peter 4:7–10)

Here the key phrase seems to be "one another"; it breathes reciprocity. Love is the power for richer relationships among believers. It works toward this end by "covering" (which probably means "forgiving")[4] the sins of others. This in turn has the effect of bringing people together physically in a setting of mutual care (hospitality) so that each one can practice his or her charisma as a gift to the others. Quite similar thinking occurs in Eph., ch. 4, where the writer states that Christ's gifts to the church—apostles, prophets, evangelists, pastors, and teachers—have been bestowed "for the equipment of the saints, for the work of ministry, for building up the body of Christ, until we all attain to the unity of the faith" (Eph. 4:11–13). He then goes on to amplify this assertion:

> Speaking the truth in love, we are to grow up in every way into him who is the head, into Christ, from whom the whole body, joined and knit together by every joint with which it is supplied, when each part is working properly, makes bodily growth and upbuilds itself in love. (Eph. 4:15–16)

Individual believers are to speak sound teachings to one another in love so that the whole community, employing its gifts in mutual ministry, may grow, building itself up *in love*. The phrase "in love" *(en agapē)* is an important one for the Ephesian writer. Apart from this passage he uses it in Eph. 1:5; 3:17; 4:2; and 5:2. The last text, in fact, furnishes us with the first subheading for our chapter: "Walk in love, as Christ loved us and gave himself up for us, a fragrant offering and sacrifice to God." Throughout Ephesians, "in love" refers to something more than the caring attitude that believers must show toward one another. It means at the same time the power behind this attitude, the inspiration for it which comes from God or Christ. The writer prays for his readers

> that Christ may dwell in your hearts through faith; that you, being rooted and grounded *in love,* may have power to comprehend with all the saints what is the breadth and length and height and depth, and to know the love of Christ which surpasses knowledge. (Eph. 3:17–19, italics added)

Once we receive Christ's love into our inner selves and have our vision expanded to contemplate its glory, then we ourselves can love others (Eph. 4:2). That is what the writer seems to be saying.[5] Walking in love therefore means not only practicing love but also keeping in touch with that power from God which inhabits and surrounds us. The notion of love in Ephesians may be used to interpret our diagram more fully. On the figure, God's love exists at nearly every point. It resides in the overarching, sustaining hemispheres. It pulsates in the large arrows left and right which push us into action, and in the vertical downward arrows which symbolize God's specific approaches to us in midstream insofar as we are conscious of them. As we move fluidly among gift, task, and Giver we literally walk "in love."

This discussion may seem terribly mystical to some readers— which is to say, removed from everyday life. Mystical it may be, but Christian experience has proved it eminently practical as well. Elizabeth O'Connor, veteran of many gift-evoking small groups at The Church of the Saviour in Washington, D.C., writes: "In the end, we have to say that the exercising of gifts has to do with love, which is a reciprocal relationship. We are addressed by love, and we love."[6] The love of which she speaks cannot be limited to the atmosphere of mutual concern which exists in the groups. It is also God's love. Each group practices meditation on the Bible, as well as private and intercessory prayer so as to nourish itself with this vertical *agapē*. Moreover, all members receive encouragement and guidance from a person within the group designated as pastor-prophet who interprets the traditional language about God for them as they struggle to identify and exercise their gifts.[7] Only through such attention to God's work in the process, O'Connor and her associates have found, can there be any movement through the discovery of gifts to corporate growth and concrete ethical action.

But let us return now to one last New Testament text about love —indeed, to the most famous one of all: I Cor., ch. 13. Paul chooses to insert this hymn, which he may have composed earlier or learned from other believers, between a description of charismata (I Cor., ch. 12) and a set of guidelines for their use (I Cor., ch. 14).

Why? Probably because he thinks of love as a necessary bridge between gift and task in much the same way that the writers of I Peter and Ephesians do. He calls love a "more excellent way" (I Cor. 12:31) and urges his readers to make it their aim as they "earnestly desire the *pneumatika*" (I Cor. 14:1). Chapter 13 itself concentrates primarily upon a love for neighbors which directs the powerful charismata toward the welfare of others. In effect, it commends love as a restraint upon the haughtiness and selfishness into which gift-filled believers may fall (I Cor. 13:1–7; see also II Cor. 5:14). Paul never calls love a charisma or a *pneumatikon*. These spiritual gifts serve to differentiate believers. They are bestowed through the Spirit "to each one individually as he wills" (I Cor. 12:11). Some believers enjoy higher gifts than others. This is not so with love, which comes to all, in equal measure, from God. Love works toward unity, toward the leveling of all superiorities and inferiorities among believers. It is freer than the gifts, which become internalized by particular believers. Therefore it must be considered "more excellent" than the gifts. It rules them. Paul does not say so explicitly, but he surely inclines toward the view that someone with lesser gifts who walks easily in love would be accomplishing God's will better than a person filled with charismata who tends to resist the demands of love (I Cor. 13:1–3; see also Mark 9:33–35). On the other hand, Paul clearly urges his readers to seek the best of all possible combinations: love *plus* the higher gift of prophecy (I Cor. 14:1).

Love constitutes the way along which we travel reciprocally from gift to task to Giver. It is a way that both requires our energy and enfolds us in an energy greater than our own. Yet we do not discern or follow love easily; no one walks its road "naturally." That is where the Spirit enters—once again. The Spirit works as a pathfinder to blaze a trail for love: "God's love has been poured into our hearts through [the agency of] the Holy Spirit which has been given to us" (Rom. 5:5). Here Paul probably refers to conversion, but the Spirit's attempts to keep love in us and us in love by no means stop there. It is constantly on the job, drawing us close to the love of God:

It is the Spirit himself bearing witness with our spirit that we are children of God, and if children, then heirs. . . .

Likewise, the Spirit helps us in our weakness; for we do not know how to pray as we ought, but the Spirit himself intercedes for us with sighs too deep for words. And he who searches the hearts of men knows what is the mind of the Spirit, because the Spirit intercedes for the saints according to the will of God. (Rom. 8:16; 26f.)

Now we have received not the spirit of the world, but the Spirit which is from God, that we might understand the gifts bestowed on us by God. (I Cor. 2:12)

On the basis of these passages and others, John Taylor appropriately names the Holy Spirit as "the Go-Between God."[8] The Spirit's reciprocal activity also shows itself in relationships among believers, that is, in the movement from gift to task. According to Paul, the preeminent "fruit" of the Spirit within believers is love for others (Gal. 5:22). Even apart from the charismata of God which the Spirit distributes to each believer (I Cor. 12:11), it labors to cultivate this way of love in everyone so that the gifts will reach their proper destination. Paul was probably not the first believer to recognize the ethical dimensions of the Spirit, but within the New Testament he certainly explicates them more fully than anyone else.

When he urges the Galatians to "walk by the Spirit" (*pneumati peripateite,* Gal. 5:16; or *pneumati stoichōmen,* Gal. 5:25), he is not talking about a pleasant feeling of closeness to God. Instead, he is telling his readers quite straightforwardly to love their neighbors as themselves, to become servants of one another through love (Gal. 5:13–16). Paul conceives of mature believers as *pneumatikoi,* "spiritual ones," who respond wholeheartedly to the Spirit's guidance (I Cor. 2:13, 15; 3:1; 14:37; Gal. 6:1). Some of the Corinthians considered themselves *pneumatikoi* (I Cor. 14:37). On the whole, I Corinthians suggests that this word—which may have been used in pagan circles as well—generally meant people with special gifts and privileges. Paul probably accepted this prevailing definition as partially correct. But whenever he got the chance, he injected a distinctively moral potion into the term. We see this clearly in two passages from his letters:

> But I, brethren, could not address you as spiritual men *(pneumatikoi),* but as men of the flesh, as babes in Christ. I fed you with milk, not solid food; for you were not ready for it; and even yet you are not ready, for you are still of the flesh. For while there is still jealousy and strife among you, are you not of the flesh, and behaving like ordinary men? (I Cor. 3:3f.; see also 14:37)

> If we live by the Spirit, let us also walk by the Spirit. Let us have no self-conceit, no provoking of one another, no envy of one another.
> Brethren, if a man is overtaken in any trespass, you who are spiritual *(pneumatikoi)* should restore him in a spirit of gentleness. Look to yourself, lest you too be tempted. Bear one another's burdens and so fulfill the law of Christ. (Gal. 5:25 to 6:2)

For Paul, there can be no true spirituality without loving action. These two passages feed our suspicion that Paul would honor a minimally gifted person who loved well over a more gifted person who loved little. The first he could address as a *pneumatikos,* since that person would be following the Spirit's lead with his or her gifts. Ironically, the second, who might enjoy more or greater charismata, could only be called a "babe in Christ." The mark of a real *pneumatikos* is the power to restore others with gentleness and humility (Gal. 6:1).

This passion for a *moral* spirituality, issuing in concrete acts of love for others, comes through forcefully in the New Testament (see, besides Paul, Matt. 5:44; 22:37–40; 25:31–46; Luke 10:29–37; John 15:8–9; Eph. 2:10; 4:25 to 5:2; II Tim. 1:6f.; Heb. 10:19–25; James 2:8–26; I John 3:16–18, 23f.; 4:7–12, 19ff.). We might well ask ourselves whether many of our discussions today about spiritual gifts do not miss the point entirely. To be sure, the New Testament writers felt extraordinarily gifted. For them, however, the chief thing was never giftedness itself or how one felt about it, but rather what one did with it. We can argue endlessly about which believers among us are the most spiritual and which offer us the best methods for attaining spirituality. But unless we infuse our talk with solid concern for ministry, our seeking will become perverse. "Make love your aim, and earnestly desire the spiritual gifts." (I Cor. 14:1.) Ideally, the two searches proceed simultaneously. But there should be no doubt that the "desire" serves the "aim" and not vice versa. Certainly we cannot love others unless we know something of God's love for us. The question is, How much of God's love do we need to know experientially before we attempt to obey him? Times will come when we must act spiritually, that is, with love toward our neighbor, when we do not feel Spirit-filled, or even loving. No doubt we shall fail, but in our failure we may learn much about charismata. They may emerge precisely in our hollowness or our pain, as they did for Paul. For some of us today, the best way to receive charismata may be to forget about them altogether as desirable stages in our upward spiritual developments and enter, more then ever before, into intense, loving conversations with God on behalf of the suffering world. If in our praying we receive or rediscover charismata, we can be sure that they will soon reveal themselves further in urgent tasks. By their fruits we shall know them. That is what walking by the Spirit means.

Some readers may wonder whether the New Testament teaching about gifts and tasks offers sufficient guidance for the fearsome technological, multinational problems we face today. Is it not true that the New Testament ethic limits itself largely to interpersonal relations and even then mostly to problems within the church, as opposed to those in society as a whole? We do face a genuine difficulty here. Written to small struggling communities, most of whom expected Christ's world-transforming return in the near future, the New Testament shows no inclination toward spelling out detailed programs for societal reform. Even the exhortations to love one's neighbors and enemies (Mark 12:31 and parallels; Matt. 5:44; Rom. 13:14), to do good to all people (Gal. 6:10), and to serve the Christ incognito in his suffering brothers and sisters (Matt. 25:31–46) represent essentially the interaction of individuals and small groups. Nor, in my view, does Jesus' teaching about the

Kingdom of God provide a helpful blueprint for societal action in today's complex world. According to the Gospels it is always God who brings in the Kingdom, not human beings who build it.

Lately, however, the lay theologian William Stringfellow has mounted a forceful argument for employing the book of Revelation as a prophetic diagnosis of the American political situation. In *An Ethic for Christians and Other Aliens in a Strange Land,* Stringfellow bypasses the currently popular allegorizations of Revelation (i.e., attempts to discover in virtually every passage explicit predictions of events in our day) and rejects as arrogance the notion that an American apocalypse must necessarily coincide with the end of the world. Instead, he attempts to expose, via the Biblical text, the pervasive power of death at work in every level of American culture, even prior to Watergate. For Stringfellow, America must be seen as the Babylon/Rome of Rev., ch. 18, not because it is inherently more evil than other countries, but because abysmal, superhuman forces have taken hold of even its best intentions and perverted them. In the face of these principalities Stringfellow finds that the late-first-century saints' refusal to worship "the beast or its image" (Rev. 20:4), that is, the Roman emperor, models forth a practical social ethic of resistance against death for believers today. Resisting death demands symbolic protests like those of Martin Luther King, Jr., and the Berrigan brothers, or, on occasion, explicit involvement in revolutionary action, like Bonhoeffer's.[9] Some readers may find Stringfellow's analysis inaccurate or excessively pessimistic. For our purposes, what makes his work particularly important is his conviction that the ethic of resistance advocated operates only in conjunction with the charismatic gift of discernment. Stringfellow believes that

> discerning signs has to do with comprehending the remarkable in common happenings, with perceiving the saga of salvation within the era of the Fall. It has to do with the ability to interpret ordinary events in both eschatological connotations, to see portents of death where others find progress or success but, simultaneously, to behold tokens of the reality of the Resurrection or hope where others are consigned to confusion or despair. . . . I regard none of the charis-

matic gifts—least of all discernment—as fantastic or outlandish, but, on the contrary, as commonplace and usual marks of the Church.[10]

This is not the place for an extensive evaluation of Stringfellow's views. We cite his work because it stands in the forefront of contemporary Christian thinking about the social/political implications of charismata.[11] He has seen that God's special gifts lead, inexorably, to special tasks and that some of these tasks, at least, will bring one hard against the national policies of one's own country. Here we come full circle to the Old Testament teaching that God's Spirit operates wherever it chooses, in the public sphere as well as in the hearts of believers.

Worship

Still, the New Testament as a whole concentrates on the believing community's special office of discerning, receiving, and employing charismata among its own people and on the ensuing conversation with God within the church.[12] The church speaks to the Giver of gifts at every phase of its charismatic life. In contrast to the unbelieving world, which regards the charismata as curiosities, the church worships. Or at least it should. Already in the New Testament we find evidence of a devastating gap in the minds of some early believers between gifts and Giver. This happens most dramatically among our old friends the Corinthians. These "babes in Christ" have come to regard the presence of the Spirit in the Eucharist as a kind of deifying substance which renders all responsibility to the transcendent God obsolete (I Cor. 10:1–22; 11:17–34).[13] They have also clamored after the "different spirit" (II Cor. 11:4) proclaimed by Paul's charismatic opponents in the hope of avoiding every claim upon their lives by the God who allowed his Son to suffer in weakness and die on the cross (II Cor., chs. 10 to 13, especially 13:1–9). Characteristically, the Corinthians seek Jesus' glory through appropriating new charismata but shy away from sharing his dying which Paul claims to carry about in his body (II Cor. 4:7–12). According to the apostle, such a truncated

Christian life follows automatically when one separates Giver from gift.

To guard against this folly, Paul encourages worship. We have already noted how the apostle urges his readers to thank God in all circumstances (I Thess. 5:16ff.). These acts of thanksgiving represent much more than the expression of a pleasant emotion. They are acts of will, fresh acknowledgments of dependence upon God, renewed dedications of bodies, minds, and spirits to his purposes. When the New Testament writers speak of worship, they mean primarily the human act of presenting oneself, humbly and sacrificially—but also joyfully—before God or Christ (e.g., Matt. 28:9, 17; Mark 5:6; John 9:38; I Cor. 14:25; Heb. 11:21; Rev. 5:14; 7:11; 19:4). For Paul, worship comes to completion in physical deeds. Thus, he gives the Romans this counsel:

> Do not yield your [bodily] members to sin as instruments of wickedness, but yield yourselves to God as men who have been brought from death to life, and your members to God as instruments of righteousness. . . . For just as you once yielded your members to impurity and to greater and greater iniquity, so now yield your members to righteousness for sanctification. (Rom. 6:13, 19)

A few chapters later we find this now familiar passage:

> I appeal to you therefore, brethren, by the mercies of God, to present your bodies as a living sacrifice, holy and acceptable to God, which is your spiritual worship. Do not be conformed to this world, but be transformed by the renewal of your mind, that you may prove ["test out by action"] what is the will of God, what is good and acceptable and perfect. (Rom. 12:1f.)

In neither of these passages does Paul have in mind a private act of individual devotion. Instead, the focus is upon the congregation's corporate self-offering, probably in a service of worship. The same thought surfaces when Paul holds up the example of the generous Macedonian churches to his Corinthian readers. Unlike the Corinthians, who were dragging their feet about completing the collection of money for poor believers in Jerusalem, these zealous people had begged "for the favor of taking part in the relief of the saints—and this, not as we expected, but first they gave themselves to the Lord and to us by the will of God" (II Cor. 8:4f.).

In all three passages worship, inspired by God's gift-giving, moves believers toward activity in the world. This we can understand. But let us note, pragmatically inclined twentieth-century folk that we are, how the movement from gift to task proves to be more than horizontal. According to Paul, it always exhibits a vertical dimension as well. In "their abundance of joy and extreme poverty" the Macedonians felt unusually gifted *by God* (II Cor. 8: 2). Therefore, they responded at once—but not with a committee meeting to appropriate money for the Jerusalem project. The first thing they did was to worship: "they gave themselves to the Lord." What does this mean? Since Paul wholeheartedly endorses the Macedonians' sense of priorities, it must mean that in his view worship represents no detour on the way to social action. Indeed, the apostle seems to think that God bestows his gifts first of all to bring believers into a consciously closer relationship with him, to strengthen their trust in his nourishing Lordship (II Cor. 1:9f.). If Paul is right, God really does desire personal thanks, expressed in definite moments of corporate self-offering (Rom. 12:1). From these, service to others follows necessarily.

The point is almost too simple—some would say too pietistic. Thus we tend to waltz over it lightly or skip it altogether. Apparently God wants our praises prior to anything else. It does not quite ring true to say that our moral actions suffice to thank him. He wants a response that notices him. That usually requires words or songs or prayers, as well as good deeds. Moreover, he wants this *often* (I Thess. 5:16–18; Phil. 4:4; Eph. 5:19f.). Paul is surely thinking of something more frequent and prolonged than a Sunday-morning nod to the Almighty when he urges us to present our bodies as a living sacrifice. If the renewal of minds resulting from this sacrifice (Rom. 12:2) can be identified with the renewal of the "inner man" described in II Cor. 4:16,[14] then it happens "every day." Without doubt, some times before God are more intense and/or extended than others. We may speculate that for many early believers the Eucharist represented one of the more profound moments since it required self-examination as well as a heightened discernment of and communion with Christ's body (I Cor. 11:

27–32).[15] Paul also suggests that husbands and wives might want to abstain from sexual intercourse "for a season that you may devote yourselves to prayer" (I Cor. 7:5). There must have been many such times when believers turned their minds toward heaven, away from a debilitatingly flat view of reality (I Cor. 2:9–12; II Cor. 4:18; Phil. 3:19f.; 4:8; I Thess. 5:4–10). Paul obviously wants these moments to multiply for his readers. He tells the Corinthians that he gives them his apostolic advice about the relative merits of marriage and celibacy "to secure your undivided devotion to the Lord" (I Cor. 7:35). The apostle sees no conflict between this strategy and his constant emphasis upon moral behavior in the world.

Worship, then, means repeated, willed submissions to God in response to his gifts. The charismata, gratefully received, renew our identities as people of God. We cannot overstress this. The early believers actually did spend a good deal of their time in conscious, thankful communion with God and Christ. If we find their behavior odd or impractical or impossible for us, we must recognize how much we differ from them.

Clearly, we have left much unsaid about worship. In tying it so closely to gifts, we dare not forget that it also happens in times of hollowness: Jesus' anguished prayer in Gethsemane (Mark 14:32 and parallels) and his cry of dereliction from the cross (Mark 15:34 and parallels); Paul's protest against his thorn in the flesh (II Cor. 12:8–10) and his moans of despair in an Asian jail (II Cor. 1:8f.); the sighing of Spirit-filled believers (in tongues!) in concert with creation's groaning (Rom. 8:22–26). All these constitute genuine worship because they transpire in the presence of God.

We can draw near to God wherever we are emotionally or vocationally. If we feel overwhelmed by a task, he is there. If we get lost somewhere between gift and task, with no consciousness of either, or of him, he will respond to our cries for help. He demands only one thing: we must be ready to hear and submit to the answer (James 4:7f.). But that is exactly the attitude required of believers who approach God full of gifts, with joy and thanksgiving (Rom. 12:1ff.). No matter how full or empty we are, no matter how spiritual or fleshly, he always stands over against us as the One who wants to give more. That is why we worship. And that is why the prayer Jesus taught continues as the archetypal model for Christian petition down through the ages: "Give us this day our daily bread."

That You May Abound

Each believer needs the daily bread of God's gifts—if for no other reason than to face up to God's enormous expectations. Life in Christ, as conceived by the New Testament authors, offers no changeless, comfortable shelter. If every day brings gifts from God, it also thrusts tremendous challenges before all who want to be disciples.

Let us take a deep breath and confront what the New Testament has to say about how we are to "work out" our salvation. While affirming the validity of their readers' present stance in faith, the canonical writers, with one voice, call upon them to give more liberally of their resources (II Cor. 9:6–10; Mark 4:24), to grow into wholeness (Matt. 5:48) and maturity (I Cor. 3:6–9; Eph. 4:13–15; Phil. 3:15; I Peter 2:2), to rekindle the Spirit within them (II Tim. 1:6), and to desire the higher charismata (I Cor. 12:31; 14:1). They are to devote themselves totally to the Lord (I Cor. 7:35), seek God's kingdom (Matt. 6:33; Col. 3:1f.), pursue love (I Cor. 14:1) while practicing it "more and more" (Phil. 1:9; I Thess. 3:12; 4:10), multiply deeds of righteousness (Matt. 5:20; II Cor. 8:7; 9:8ff.; Phil. 1:11; 4:17; Col. 1:10; Heb. 10:25). They are asked to take on a larger share of Christ's suffering (II Cor. 1:5–7; Phil. 3:10–15), abound in thanksgiving (II Cor. 4:15; 9:12; Col. 2:7), increase in knowledge and discernment (Phil. 1:9; Col. 1:9–10; II Peter 3:18), build up the body of Christ more effectively (I Cor. 14:12; Eph. 4:11–16), and progress in faith (II Cor. 10:15; Phil. 1:25).

Paul sums it all up when he exhorts the Corinthians to be "always abounding in the work of the Lord" (I Cor. 15:58). Even reading this list consumes vast quantities of energy! To what degree the original recipients of the New Testament books achieved these goals, we cannot say. The point is that they now stand in the canonical text for *our* guidance. If we have been correct in reading the New Testament as a book about the abundant giving of God, then we must conclude that these high exhortations have not been written to make us feel guilty for our manifold deficiencies but rather to encourage us in the hope that we can become much more than we are.

The question is, How? Paul actually has an answer for it. He always reminds his readers that they are *already* God's children (Rom. 8:15ff.; Gal. 4:4–7), God's field, and God's building (I Cor. 3:9; 6:19). This means that he is presently at work in them (Phil. 2:13) even when they do not perceive him. In the end, "only God gives the growth" (I Cor. 3:7), and he labors mightily to achieve it—through the charismata. Something about these mysterious gifts leads believers forward in thought and action; through recognizing and practicing them we respond "more and more" to God's call "to the life above" (Phil. 3:14, NEB, TEV). Paul spells this out in a programmatic passage written to the Corinthians:

> Now we did not receive the spirit of the world, but the Spirit which is from God, in order that we might come to a deeper knowledge of the gifts bestowed on us by God *(ta charisthenta)*. Likewise, the things that we apostles say, we speak not in words taught by human wisdom but in those taught by the Spirit, as we interpret spiritual gifts *(pneumatika)* to spiritual people *(pneumatikois)*. (I Cor. 2:12f., author's translation)[16]

Here Paul sees the Spirit's task, and his own, as that of teaching believers what their gifts mean. He says much the same thing in Rom. 12:1–8 when he urges his readers to submit to a constant transformation of their minds so that they may grow in their understanding of what roles their charismata are to play in the life of the congregation. According to II Cor. 3:18, this transformation is a work of the Spirit. In its context the passage from I Corinthians, ch. 2, conveys Paul's hope that the proud Corinthians will learn something about the gift of the cross (see I Cor. 1:18 to 2:5). But we may find other, equally valid, messages in this text. The word translated "come to a deeper knowledge of" *(eidōmen)* also means "understand," "recognize," or "experience."[17] In other words, one may already have charismata, even *pneumatika* (I Cor.

2:13), that one does not yet know in an experiential way. The neo-Pentecostal clergyman Erwin Prange must have discovered this, for he tells his own story of spiritual renewal under the title *The Gift Is Already Yours.*[18] When we add to this teaching Paul's conviction that the Spirit inhabits all believers, thereby making each one charismatic, we may discern a word of God for our time. If the Corinthians, who manifested all the charismata listed in I Cor., chs. 12 to 14, needed to learn more about their gifts, then we, who perhaps have never even gotten personally acquainted with our charismata, can expect to receive much prodding from the Spirit. The Pauline injunctions to seek the "higher gifts" (I Cor. 12:31; 14:1), taking care not to "quench" the Spirit (I Thess. 5:19), may apply quite directly to our condition.

Here we must pause to make clear that the interpretation just presented ought not to be taken as an endorsement of contemporary Pentecostal or neo-Pentecostal theology, or as a call to affiliate with such groups.[19] In the New Testament, glossolalia does not function as a necessary rite of passage to the higher charismata such as prophecy, interpretation, or wisdom. God may bestow whatever charismata he pleases in any way he pleases. The ways recorded are numerous: conversation about and response to the word of God, prayer for oneself or others, loving action in which believers extend themselves beyond their apparent resources, situations of danger for the church, or the testing of believers by secular authorities. Likewise, the New Testament reveals many ways of walking in love, by the Spirit, many ways of offering ourselves up to God in worship. No theological position or community holds a monopoly on the charismata.

We are calling ourselves to take seriously—and the weight of the New Testament stands behind that call—the gifts, known, unknown, or undeveloped, which God has already granted to us. We could, at this very moment, give of our resources more extravagantly than we do, because we have within us more of God's gifts than we imagine. "By the power at work within us [he] is able to do far more abundantly than all that we ask or think." (Eph. 3:20.) The difficult saying of Jesus, "To him who has will more be given" (Mark 4:25; Matt 13:12; Luke 8:18), fits in here. It probably refers to the believer who acknowledges with thanksgiving and submission before God the gifts he or she has already received. That person will continue to prosper. The passage may also mean that the believer who trades with what he or she has been given receives additional tasks, along with God's commendation. Such is the lesson that emerges from the parables of the talents (Matt. 25: 14–30) and the pounds (Luke 19:22–27). Paul elaborates on this principle of God's economy in his attempt to move the Corinthians toward completing their part of the collection for Jerusalem:

> The point is this: he who sows sparingly will also reap sparingly, and he who sows bountifully will also reap bountifully. Each one must do as he has made up his mind, not reluctantly or under compulsion, for God loves a cheerful giver. And God is able to provide you with every blessing in abundance, so that you may always have enough of everything and may provide in abundance for every good work. As it is written,
>> "He scatters abroad, he gives to the poor;
>> his righteousness endures for ever."
> He who supplies seed to the sower and bread for food will supply and multiply your resources and increase the harvest of your righteousness. (II Cor. 9:6–10)

The question, How shall we abound? can be translated into another one: How shall we seek, find, and practice our charismata? The New Testament furnishes no simple answer. But it does offer us considerable guidance. We have learned, for example, that every search for charismata will sooner or later encounter the cross. We need not be surprised if the joyous discovery of a gift brings with it a larger share in Christ's sufferings. Paul would call that progress in faith. We have also learned that charismata can be quiet experiences as well as spectacular and excitable ones.[20] Moreover, one can practice them without fear of uncontrolled possession by the Spirit.

Still another New Testament teaching speaks with unusual force. It speaks especially to those of us who feel drawn by the Biblical commands and promises toward a charismatic understanding of who we are and what we are to do, but find ourselves skeptical about contemporary groups that call themselves charismatic. The teaching we refer to concerns Christian community. We observed in Chapter 4 that according to the canonical writers, charismata appear almost exclusively when believers or prospective believers assemble in groups. They seem to require, as well as create, a sense of corporate personality. Likewise, with one exception (II Tim. 1:6) the numerous exhortations cited above are all directed to congregations. The New Testament writers propose to measure growth in faith not so much by taking the spiritual pulses of individuals—this is our peculiar Western bias—as by examining what happens in a community and in the world immediately surrounding that community. Biblically speaking, one gauges the number, quality, and effectiveness of the spiritual gifts *per congregation.*

But how many communities do we know, congregational or otherwise, where the primary objectives are to speak with God and one another about our gifts and tasks? In many of our churches Christian hospitality has become a lost art. Too frequently we meet together only for institutional maintenance, for anesthetic escape from the rigors of the day, and even for psychic competition. What would happen if, in the *midst* of such a gathering someone suggested that all activity cease for a moment while we submitted our present concerns to the Lord?

The New Testament counsels us, quite simply, to speak with one another about the mysteries of giftedness. Whether that happens in Sunday morning worship, in meetings of the church council, in small prayer groups, in task forces for social action, in Bible study, or when believers meet one another around the dinner table makes no difference at all. The only requirement is that God be a partner to the conversation and that all the human participants be helped to discover, practice, and understand their charismata more deeply. It seems unnecessary to label such meetings charismatic or uncharismatic. If we have learned anything from this study, it is that Paul's reflections about charismata shatter our narrow definitions. The communities here envisioned are nothing other than "places" where Christians can do what they have always done when they listen to the Spirit and the Scriptures: seek, share, learn, love, pray, and work.

Probably we ought to refrain from setting rigid agendas for such "free spaces."[21] We can, however, look for signs that something redemptive is happening. And here the New Testament gives us intriguing models to heighten our discernment:

> And they devoted themselves to the apostles' teaching and fellowship, to the breaking of bread and the prayers. (Acts 2:42)

> If all prophesy, and an unbeliever or outsider enters, he is convicted by all, . . . the secrets of his heart are disclosed; and so, falling on his face, he will worship God and declare that God is really among you. (I Cor. 14:24f.)

> Do not get drunk with wine, for that is debauchery; but be [keep on being] filled with the Spirit, addressing one another in psalms and hymns and spiritual songs, singing and making melody to the Lord with all your heart, always and for everything giving thanks in the name of our Lord Jesus Christ to God the Father. (Eph. 5:18–20)

> Above all hold unfailing your love for one another, since love covers a multitude of sins. Practice hospitality ungrudgingly to one another. As each has received a gift *(charisma),* employ it for one another, as good stewards of God's varied grace *(charis):* whoever speaks, as one who utters oracles of God; whoever renders service, as one who renders it by the strength which God supplies; in order that in everything God may be glorified through Jesus Christ. (I Peter 4:8–11)

Let us grant the last word in this discussion of gifts, tasks, and Giver to Paul. After calling upon the Roman congregation to offer itself up thankfully to God so that individual believers may learn more fully how to put their varied charismata to work for others, the apostle moves immediately into what looks at first reading like simple-minded advice:

> Let love be genuine; hate what is evil, hold fast to what is good; love one another with brotherly affection; outdo one another in showing honor. Never flag in zeal, be aglow with the Spirit, serve the Lord. Rejoice in your hope, be patient in tribulation, be constant in prayer. Contribute to the needs of the saints, practice hospitality.
>
> Bless those who persecute you; bless and do not curse them. Rejoice with those who rejoice, weep with those who weep. Live in harmony with one another; do not be haughty, but associate with

the lowly [or, as the RSV alternate reading has it: "give yourselves to humble tasks"]; never be conceited. Repay no one evil for evil, but take thought for what is noble in the sight of all. If possible, so far as it depends upon you, live peaceably with all. (Rom. 12:9–18)

Paul appears to be working out what a congregation would look like, practically, if it exercised its charismata faithfully for the neighbor before God. If our meetings together embodied just one of these "simple-minded" virtues, we would probably experience blessing beyond measure.

CHAPTER 7

Charismata and Charismatics

Nine centuries ago Anselm of Canterbury defended his speculative theological writings before critics who questioned their propriety. He argued that Christian faith inevitably seeks understanding. It was a good defense, for it dovetails smoothly with Paul's conviction that God gives us the Spirit in order to help us understand what he has given us! (I Cor. 2:12). Like a teacher, the Spirit interprets both itself and the charismata which it distributes (I Cor. 2:13).

All believers, including the fully charismatic Corinthians, according to Paul, need constant growth in comprehension. In some ways this need begins to be met by the gifts themselves, for charismata create within their recipients a passion for learning. Once people discover their charismata and begin to practice them, however tentatively and clumsily, they always want to know what is happening to them with their minds as well as their hearts. They want to match their new experiences with what they have learned about life up until then, reaffirming some of it as truth and discarding some as error. They want to talk about their experiences of God's grace both with those who seem to understand what it means and with those who do not, but may wish to. All this requires a framework of disciplined thinking, for only that allows a person to translate his or her deepest stirrings into a common language. We are not talking about intellectual mastery over a body of inert data. Understanding our charismata means recognizing anew who we are and what we are to do with our gifts before a transcendent God

(Rom. 12:1–8). To put it another way, the person who discovers a charisma stands at the beginning of a process. It is a process that involves not only savoring the gift with joy and thanksgiving, but also exercising it and then attempting to comprehend what happens as a result of that effort. From this attempt may follow further seeking, repeated acts of submission, the granting of new charismata, or even painful perplexity at the mysteries of God (II Cor. 4:8). But according to Paul, this too counts as a form of "understanding."

What we are saying is that through the charismata we already have, God's Spirit will lead us into new conclusions about the nature of reality. Gifts perceived demand activity, and not least the activity of the mind.

Here our study of the New Testament material brings us up against the teachings and practices of contemporary Pentecostal and neo-Pentecostal believers. Let us try to be as clear as possible about the nature of this collision. On the positive side, much of our investigation has in fact confirmed as Biblical the experiences that Pentecostals report. We do not exaggerate in agreeing with them that every major New Testament author presupposes widespread charismatic events among the believers he addresses. The notion of giftedness plays an absolutely central role in the feeling and thinking of the canonical writers. Together, they assume that all believers will enjoy some consciousness of the Spirit's refreshing presence in their lives, as well as a pressure to conform their wills more and more to the will of God as revealed in the Spirit's proddings. Luke and the writer to the Ephesians speak of repeated infusions of the Spirit which result in a heightened (if temporary) sense of fullness or nearness to God. Paul himself does not explicitly recommend a filling with the Spirit, but neither does he denounce the experience as illusory.[1] On the contrary, he approaches Lucan and Ephesian language when he affirms that "God's love has been poured into our hearts through the Holy Spirit which has been given to us" (Rom. 5:5); when he urges his Roman readers to keep themselves "aglow with the Spirit" (Rom. 12:11); and when he prays that God may "fill [them] with all joy and peace in believing, so that by the power of the Holy Spirit [they] may abound in hope" (Rom. 15:

13; see also II Cor. 7:4 and Phil. 4:18f.). Finally, for the record, our study compels us to stand with Pentecostals and neo-Pentecostals in opposing a view often articulated by dispensationalist Christians. It is that God has by and large restricted charismatic phenomena to the first century when such spectacular events were needed for the missionary expansion of the young church. Nothing in the New Testament even remotely suggests that charismata might be *replaced* by the spoken or written word once the church had decided upon its Scriptural canon. By picturing the earliest church as an ideal charismatic community, Luke probably wishes to stir up the practice of spiritual gifts among his late-first-century readers.[2] In several respects, therefore, contemporary Pentecostal believers have shown themselves better interpreters of the Bible than many of their highly educated counterparts in the traditional denominations.

Nevertheless, charismatic *experience* alone does not suffice as a faithful enactment of the gospel preached by the New Testament writers. A careful, Scriptural *interpretation* of the charismata must also follow. Here we come full circle to the collision we mentioned above. Contemporary Pentecostals and neo-Pentecostals can hardly be faulted for neglecting the interpretation of their gifts. Their personal testimonies, conferences, books, and tape cassettes abound. But our study has raised the question of whether their understanding of the gifts granted them remains as true to the teaching of the New Testament as their nonrational experience appears to be. The conclusions reached in our previous chapters suggest that some types of current Pentecostal and neo-Pentecostal thinking ought to be seen as misinterpretations of genuine works of the Spirit. To these we now turn.

The Dangers of Misinterpretation

In contrast to Paul, who found joy in the midst of suffering, some Pentecostals and neo-Pentecostals seek happiness to the exclusion of all other human experiences. We can understand this urge. The first discovery of charismata usually brings with it a flood of positive emotions. The New Testament writers certainly know and affirm such moments of elation. The danger comes in identifying the charisma or the Spirit of God with these pleasant feelings. When the gift tends to merge with one's human response to it, the gift can no longer stand over against its recipient to comfort and to challenge. But worse than this, God and the Spirit may be banished by charismatically gifted persons from their emotional troughs. In extreme cases one ends up saying something like: "Unless I can regularly feel the way I did on that day when I was baptized in the Spirit, the whole business, including God, must be phony."[3] Or: "Since I now find myself in the depths, God must have left me and taken his charisma with him. What grievous sin have I committed? What must I do to bring them back?" We might call this kind of thinking an "underinterpretation" of the charismata. It fails to recognize the charismatic presence of God at the heart of suffering and therefore rejects the gift of the cross. One gives up deep joy in order to chase after shallow happiness. To their credit, seasoned Pentecostals have shown themselves very much aware of this problem.[4] We would not need to dwell upon it here except that it sometimes leads to an even more serious "overinterpretation" of charismatic experience.

We refer to the potentially tyrannical prescription of stages in spiritual growth. The higher plateaus are popularly associated with ever more pleasant emotions. Because Pentecostal and neo-Pentecostal theology concentrates its gaze so intently upon the spectacular reversals that often take place initially in the lives of charismatically gifted individuals, it tends to devise "normative" sequences of experience through which true believers ought to pass if they want to become more spiritual. First is a dramatic baptism in the Spirit by the risen Christ (to be distinguished from water baptism in which one completes one's coming to faith via the Spirit's working). Then is a confirmation of this baptism through the practice of glossolalia and a resulting condition called the Spirit-filled life. Further sanctification is often accompanied by the granting of other charismata.

We have discovered some truth in this pattern, especially the last element. But we have also found that the New Testament never hardens any such cluster of events into a norm against which believers must constantly measure themselves to find out whether they are progressing satisfactorily. Further, we have maintained that according to the New Testament a baptism in the Spirit apart from water baptism cannot be regarded as typical. Hence, we regard the central Pentecostal and neo-Pentecostal teaching as an overinterpretation. The danger of such a teaching is manifest when Pentecostally oriented believers within a traditional congregation "invite" non-Pentecostals to share in their newfound spiritual riches. In itself, this is a fine practice, well documented in the New Testament (Rom. 1:11f.; I Peter 4:9–11). Often, however, the invitation carries a hidden clause. It reads not, "Come as you are and enjoy the treasure I have been granted," but "Come and become like me, since only then will you enjoy God's higher blessings." In other words, one finds acceptance for what one may be transformed into, not for what one is.[5] This approach fails to do justice both to God's sovereignty in granting charismata however he pleases and to Paul's conviction that every believer has his or her "own special gift *(charisma)* from God, one of one kind and one of another" (I Cor. 7:7).

In this context we must also register a vigorous protest against the term "Spirit-filled" when Pentecostals and neo-Pentecostals use it to distinguish themselves from other believers. Are others Spirit-empty? Spirit-half-filled? Our study of the New Testament data has revealed that Luke and the writer to the Ephesians think of indivdiuals as being filled repeatedly by the Spirit. For these authors, believers do not remain Spirit-filled just because they have undergone a particular experience. One must receive the Spirit's fullness again and again on specific occasions, sometimes in worship, sometimes in crisis situations (Eph. 5:18ff.; Acts 4:23–31; 6:5–10; 7:55). To put it curtly, no one except Jesus may claim to live in a continuous state of spiritual fullness. All believers, including non-Pentecostals, may expect to enjoy this fullness from time to time. In the New Testament a *pneumatikos,* or "spiritual person," is one who follows the Spirit's lead, particularly in his or her moral behavior, not one who constantly bubbles over with positive emotions.

Another tendency to which some Pentecostals and neo-Pentecostals succumb is an unnecessarily wooden Biblical literalism. Again, we can understand why someone who has discovered the experiential reality of what more rationalistic believers shrug off as naive first-century language for "natural" phenomena would tend to read the Bible on a realistic level. But Biblical realism can hardly be equated with Biblical literalism. Realism is found in the common, harmonious witness borne by the various authors to Jesus as the Christ. It also appears in the conflicts that exist, for example, among the three synoptic accounts of Jesus' ministry, or between Paul and John on the question of eschatology. Indeed, Paul's letters, taken as a whole, show that Paul himself did not always achieve consistency on some issues. Like any other dynamic leader, he sometimes changed his mind or gave directions that appear to contradict other directions, because he wrote them to specific needs which he never envisioned as existing in all places at all times. Thus the developments and tensions in a particular author's thought also count as part of canonical truth. Paul would surely find ridiculous any effort to harmonize all his statements on every theme.

Let us examine two areas of Biblical interpretation in which some Pentecostally oriented believers seem to have derived more than they should from the wisdom granted them in their charismata. One is the Biblical view of male-female relationships. The neo-Pentecostal author of a popular guidebook to Christian family life insists, for example, on a clearly defined chain of command within the family where the man acts as "head" in a way analogous to Christ's Lordship over the church (Eph. 5:23–27).[6] Interpreters who take this position are quick to point out that the husband's lordship must be exercised lovingly and sacrificially, like Christ's, and that spouses must submit to each other in certain matters (Eph. 5:21, 25–33). Still they tend to favor texts in the Deutero-Pauline literature that highlight woman's submission to man (Eph. 5:22–24; Col. 3:18; I Tim. 2:9–15; Titus 2:3–5).[7] Neo-Pentecostals sometimes refer to female subordination as an order of creation intended by God from the beginning (Gen. 2:21–23). At other times they take their cue from Gen. 3:16, where it is seen as a curse resulting from Eve's sin. Both views are held by the author of I Timothy, who writes:

> I permit no woman to teach or have authority over men; she is to keep silent. For Adam was formed first, then Eve; and Adam was not deceived, but the woman was deceived and became a transgressor. (I Tim. 2:12ff.)

Understandably, believers who incline toward the literal acceptance of such reasoning would have to oppose not only shared decision-making power in a marriage relationship but also women's ordination to the ministry. It is hardly accidental that women occupy almost none of the publicly acknowledged leadership positions in contemporary neo-Pentecostal communities.[8]

The genuine Pauline epistles present a much more complex view of the status of women in the earliest church than that espoused by conservative charismatic (and evangelical) believers. When Paul says in I Cor. 7:4a that "the wife does not rule over her own body but the husband does," he is echoing the conventional wisdom of Hellenistic society. But when he goes on to assert in v. 4b that "the husband does not rule over his own body but the wife does," he moves beyond subordinationist doctrine into a reciprocity that would have sounded radically egalitarian to many of his readers.[9] "In the Lord" woman enjoys a new interdependence with man quite different from the inferior status assigned her by the writer(s) of Gen., chs. 2 and 3 (see I Cor. 11:11–12). According to I Cor. 11:5, women prayed and prophesied in the worship services of the assembled church, apparently with the same charismatic authority as men. And in Gal. 3:28, Paul boldly proclaims that "there is neither Jew nor Greek, there is neither slave nor free, there is neither male nor female; for you are all one in Christ Jesus." Krister Stendahl has rightly called this text a "breakthrough" in Paul's thought where the apostle takes full notice of the revolutionary new creation (II Cor. 5:17; Gal. 6:15) as it rises to challenge the order of fallen creation even before Christ's visible return from heaven.[10] At the same time, however, perhaps to hold open the door for potential converts who might be scandalized by such a classless society, Paul does not allow his congregations to *practice* full equality between males and females. Women must wear veils when they prophesy (I Cor. 11:2–16) and, if I Cor. 14:33–36 comes from the apostle's hand, wives are to "keep silence in the churches."[11] Here we see an unresolved tension in Paul's thought. What we do with it today depends upon our principles of Biblical interpretation. Honest believers may differ.[12] Our point is that it does not follow exegetically that charismatic households or communities ought to take the Deutero-Pauline epistles as their exclusive model for the relationship between the sexes. Charismatic experience itself gives one no privileged insight into this matter. Believers overinterpret their gifts if they claim otherwise.

A second area in which Pentecostals and neo-Pentecostals may be led by their charismatic experience to distort certain Biblical material is eschatology, which literally means "the doctrine concerning last things." From its very beginning the Pentecostal movement has often displayed a heightened expectation of Christ's return from heaven. Having experienced a new outpouring of the Spirit, Pentecostal believers identify easily with Luke's Peter as he interprets his Pentecost blessing via the words of the prophet Joel:

> And in the last days it shall be, God declares,
> that I will pour out my Spirit upon all flesh,
> and your sons and your daughters shall prophesy.
> (Acts 2:17)[13]

In this intensified hope neo-Pentecostals generally follow the lead of their classical cousins. At the same time, however, there appears to be no unanimity in either group of believers as to exactly when or how the Parousia will take place. The expectations of Pentecostally oriented believers ought not to be identified with the apocalyptic fervor of, say, the Jehovah's Witnesses. To my knowledge, no modern Pentecostal group has sold all its possessions and sat down on a mountain to wait. On the other hand, especially since the late 1960's when charismatic gifts began to erupt with greater frequency in the traditional churches, neo-Pentecostal interpreters especially have attempted to understand their experience as part of a cosmic divine plan. J. Rodman Williams, Presbyterian minister/ scholar and director of the Melodyland Christian Center, has called the Spirit's work today "a new world" characterized by "the interpenetration of the spiritual and the natural." In this "era of the Spirit" we may sense "the dawning of a profound and lasting unity among brethren." According to Williams, we are compelled by the current charismatic movement to talk about eschatology:

> For when the Spirit of God is released, or poured out, the "end" of creation is at hand: the "last time" has come! [Here Williams cites Acts 2:17.] The whole of creation, long in bondage to corruption, emancipated by the saving deed of God in Christ, is thereby suffused with God's presence and power. For God's purpose does not end with redemption, wherein creation is restored to its pristine integrity, but moves on to the consummation in which God comes to His redeemed world to occupy and possess, to pervade and permeate, to fill and fulfill. With the tragic blight of evil and corruption removed, the way is clear for God to move upon and within this new reality, and to bring all things into unity with Himself.
>
> Herein is disclosed the mystery of God and the world, God and man, in completeness. God thereby becomes wholly immanent within his creation, for, while remaining the transcendent God, He nonetheless by the movement of His Spirit, claims the heights and depths of creaturely existence. This is neither the divinization of the world nor its metamorphosis into another kind of reality. It is rather the glory of God filling creation and inaugurating the transformation of all things into His own image and likeness.[14]

One of the problems with this visionary proclamation is that its timetable remains unclear. Will the end of all things come quite soon, within a few years perhaps, or by the end of the century? To what extent can we now discern and participate in such a cosmic transformation? Will great natural disasters and persecutions precede its consummation (as in I Cor. 7:26–31; II Thess. 2:1–12; Mark, ch. 13/Matt., ch. 24/Luke, ch. 21; and the book of Revelation)? Or will it unfold in relative peace on the plane of human history? Without further information one would have to guess that Williams inclines toward the second scenario.

A similar, but more Biblically sophisticated optimism emerges in *The Spirit and the World,* by James W. Jones, a neo-Pentecostal Episcopal priest and Rutgers University professor of religion.

Jones carefully distinguishes between the charismatic community of believers and God's Kingdom. He conceives of the latter as three concentric circles:

> The outer circle is the rule of God the Father in creation and providence, encompassing the whole cosmos. The middle circle is the reign of Christ, which takes place within the larger context of the divine creation and providence but will not, until the end when "all things are put in subjection under his feet" [Jones is referring to I Cor. 15:24–28], coincide with creation. Within this circle is the third and smallest one which represents the work of the Spirit—the Spirit-filled community, which acknowledges the Lordship of God the Father and the Lordship of Christ. . . . The coming of the Kingdom can be seen as the progression of the inner circle toward the outer rim until all the cosmos is subject to Christ and filled with the Spirit.[15]

According to Jones, present-day manifestations of charismatic gifts "not only give men a glimpse of the coming Kingdom but they hasten its arrival, as the sphere of the Spirit's work is enlarged."[16] The task of charismatic communities therefore becomes that of marshaling all their resources, whether conventional or extraordinary, to provide healing for the world and thus to proclaim the Kingdom's advent. Such communities, presently at work,

> are not solving the vast problems of education, urban blight, or mental illness, but they point toward the time when schools, cities, and hospitals will be communities. Within the charismatic movement and the churches at large, physicians, nurses, teachers, social workers, businessmen, truck drivers, laborers are trying to bring something of the life of the Spirit into their work and to order their lives in such a way as to allow the Spirit to create community through them. As the perimeters of submission to the work of the Spirit are enlarged, more of existence is filled with the Spirit until that day comes when the earth shall be filled with the glory of God as the waters fill up the sea.[17]

As in Williams' work the hope seems to be that the Spirit's activity in the world will move developmentally toward a final perfection. Jones adds the proviso that this process will not coincide with the progressive solution of current social/economic/political problems, but like Williams he refrains from picturing the last days as a degeneration of world order. One detects in each of these authors a view that the Spirit's work will unfurl gradually, almost smoothly, without provoking major opposition.

At the opposite end of the spectrum stands Assemblies of God (Pentecostal) minister David Wilkerson. He is well known for his best-selling book *The Cross and the Switchblade,* in which he narrates his remarkable work with street gangs in New York City. When Wilkerson appeared as a scheduled speaker at the (neo-Pentecostal) International Lutheran Conference on the Holy Spirit in August, 1973, he startled the audience by announcing that God had granted him a vision of impending doom for America. The calamities he forecast included massive economic chaos, overwhelming natural disasters, widespread sexual immorality within the church, persecution of "Spirit-filled Christians," and finally an exodus of all true believers from the hopelessly corrupt traditional churches.[18] Both the neo-Pentecostal leaders of the conference and at least one of Wilkerson's Pentecostal colleagues urged caution in accepting the vision as an authentic message from God.[19]

Apparently no unanimity exists even today among Pentecostally oriented believers as to its accuracy. Wilkerson subsequently published a more extensive version of his message in a book called *The Vision.* Then, in 1976 another book on the topic, *Racing Toward Judgment,* appeared under his name as a sequel to the first. In this second work Wilkerson attempts to ground the contents of his vision Biblically, without appeals to a privileged supernatural knowledge of the future. Wilkerson disclaims the title of prophet, preferring instead to call himself simply a "watchman." In the introduction to *Racing Toward Judgment* he writes:

> I have no sense of destiny, and I am not motivated by dreams or impressions. I have spent months studying my Bible, learning how God deals with societies and nations that forget Him. It was that long look back into historical prophecy that prompted my look into

the future. God's methods of judgment may change with each generation, but His justice never changes. Now I don't have to say, "This I prophesy." I can, with confidence, say, "This is what God will do, based on the record of His Word."[20]

As the main body of his work unfolds, it becomes apparent that Wilkerson's Biblical canon consists largely of passages gleaned from the Old Testament prophets, especially Jeremiah. He seems intent upon avoiding references to the book of Revelation and to the other apocalyptic sections of the New Testament such as I Thess, ch. 4; II Thess., ch. 2; I Cor., chs. 7 and 15; Mark, ch. 13/Matt., ch. 24/Luke, ch. 21, which deal with the order of events that will immediately precede Christ's Second Coming.[21] Wilkerson's method might indicate that he does not want his readers to confuse the alleged impending judgment upon America with the end of the world. And indeed he does hint at a distinction between the two when he writes:

> Out of the rubble [of great earthquakes] will come a praising remnant. They will be led out to safety. Should Christ's coming be delayed it will be years before there will be even a partial resemblance of the former days.[22]

But this passage is ambiguous, for we might interpret it to mean that Christ's Second Coming will *probably* occur at the time of the judgment, although it *may be* delayed. Wilkerson adds to the ambiguity when he asserts:

> God has brought this world to its final hour—the hour of decision! "Multitudes, multitudes in the valley of decision: for the day of the Lord is near in the valley of decision" (Joel 3:14, KJV). . . . Once again the Holy Spirit is calling God's people to make their final move. *We know the end is near.*[23]

Judged as a work of Biblical interpretation, Wilkerson's book falls woefully short. At crucial points he neglects to deal with what the New Testament says about judgment. At other times he sets forth quite explicit prophecies about the order of the final earthquakes, the onset of a dustbowl in the United States far worse than that of the '30s, the fate of Canadian and Australian wheat crops, the events surrounding New York City's demise, and the collapse of the Swiss banking system, yet without citing appropriately explicit Biblical texts.[24] One wonders whether he has given up his claim to private revelation after all.

Apart from these exegetical and hermeneutical difficulties, we must reckon with the confusion that results when we set Wilkerson's picture of the future over against the pictures offered by Williams and Jones. While some may wish to maintain that the two types of forecasts need not be taken as altogether contradictory, it seems clear that one would have to expend a great deal of ingenious effort to reconcile them. Would it not be better simply to say that charismatic experience, however genuine, provides no guarantee that one will see clearly into God's plan for the immediate future? It was a great charismatic indeed who wrote:

> For our knowledge is imperfect and our prophecy is imperfect.
> . . . For now we see in a mirror dimly, but then face to face. Now
> I know in part; then I shall understand fully, even as I have been
> fully understood. (I Cor. 13:9, 12)

Paul's judgment concerning the imperfection of prophecy applies to his own vision of the future. At certain stages of his ministry he frankly expected to be preserved from death until Jesus returned from heaven (I Thess. 4:13–18; I Cor. 15:51–53). He even dignified this second prediction with the solemn words, "Lo, I tell you a mystery" (v. 51), which probably means that he looked upon what he was about to say as a revelation granted to him alone.[25] To put it bluntly, Paul's interpretation of his own destiny within God's plan was at this point wrong.

Our purpose has been to point up the difficulties into which charismatic believers (including apostles!) may fall as they strive, legitimately, to understand their experience in dialogue with the Biblical tradition. We ought not to leave any impression that we are ridiculing this effort. In fact, we must consider it right and necessary (I Cor. 2:12), though subject to dangers. Nor should we think that since Pentecostals and neo-Pentecostals have sometimes misinterpreted their gifts and/or the Bible, and since their interpretations disagree with one another, we may therefore write the whole movement off as a snare and a delusion. On the contrary, our study has attempted to show that we must regard charismatic experience and the interpretation of that experience by charismatics as separable issues. The charismata manifest God's challenging power in a way that far transcends the earthen vessels into which he pours them. Those of us who have ears to hear, let us listen to what the Spirit is saying to the churches (Rev. 3:6).

Commands and Promises for the People of God

What *is* the message of the Spirit to the churches today? What is it particularly to those of us in the traditional denominations who find ourselves confused by diverse charismatic movements around us and in our midst? How can we listen attentively to the written word, as well as to God's voice in the world and the witness of the Spirit in our own hearts? How can we discern the truth for our day? We should be guilty of gross exaggeration or worse if we claimed that our study had answered these questions with total clarity. Nevertheless, certain conclusions have emerged with such impact that we cannot ignore them. Let us review them.

1. A profound sense of giftedness pervades the thinking and feeling of all the New Testament writers as they attempt to understand the fullness of time introduced by the death and resurrection of Jesus Christ.

2. Paul, with the author of I Peter following him, distinguishes certain of God's eschatological gifts as charismata. These are personalized blessings for individuals distributed among congregations of believers through the agency of the Holy Spirit. Some charismata appear quite extraordinary in their manifestation and use (e.g., prophecy, healing, miracles, tongues, etc.). Others border on what we would call talents or inclinations (e.g., administration, teaching, liberality in the contribution of money, celibacy). The lists of charismata in the New Testament cannot be considered exhaustive. Paul expected to discover new ones as his ministry progressed.

3. The major writers of the New Testament (especially Paul, John, and Luke) simply assume a familiarity on the part of their readers with the reception and practice of charismatic gifts. Luke may be writing to Christians who, in his view, are neglecting their gifts and ought therefore to take encouragement from the charismatic fullness of the earliest church and reclaim them.

4. No New Testament writer views as normative or typical a baptism in the Spirit apart from water baptism, evidence for which is seen in one's ability to speak in tongues. On the other hand, Paul and Luke do presume that believers generally receive the Spirit in connection with their water baptism. As a result of this, the Spirit will grant each believer at least one special charisma (I Cor. 7:7).

5. Believers sometimes receive and practice charismata during moments when they are "filled" with the Spirit. This filling takes place repeatedly and cannot necessarily be identified with what Pentecostals and neo-Pentecostals call baptism in the Spirit. No New Testament writer insists that believers must feel full of the Spirit in order to recognize or use their charismata. Speaking in tongues may, for example, express a feeling of emptiness (though not hopelessness).

6. Believers are to grow experientially, intellectually, and practically in their knowledge of the charismata already granted to them (I Cor. 2:12). Paul in particular urges his charismatically gifted readers to fulfill the tasks for which their gifts have equipped them. For the apostle, spirituality must issue in morality, especially love, to prove itself authentic.

7. Hand in hand with the joy surrounding charismata comes a greater share in Christ's suffering: the gift of the cross.

8. Paul exhorts even his most gifted readers to keep on seeking "higher charismata" like prophecy. They are not to compete with their neighbors in a climb up the spiritual ladder but to serve one another more graciously and effectively. Christian life inevitably means "abounding" in the work of the Lord.

9. The beginning and end of all charismata is worship: the willed offering of one's whole self to the mysterious purposes of God.

With how much of this bedrock New Testament theologizing can we identify experientially? Pentecostals and neo-Pentecostals have taught us that the practice of charismata is possible in our day. From the first century, Paul urges us to acquaint ourselves with the charismata which are already ours. What does this mean? The Holy Spirit appears to have caught us in a cross fire. We need not join Pentecostal or neo-Pentecostal communities. Nevertheless, insofar as we claim any intimacy with God through Christ, and insofar as we wish to understand that intimacy in Pauline, Lucan, or Johannine terms, we have no choice but to identify ourselves as charismatics and proceed on our Christian pilgrimage with that intriguing selfhood.

Some readers may find such a conclusion unsettling. Probably it is no more unsettling (and perhaps infinitely less so!) than the discomfort most of us already feel at having left untapped many of our best inner resources. Elizabeth O'Connor writes:

> One reason for difficulty in our lives is that others have confirmed in us the obvious or what they, themselves, wanted to see. To please them, or to get ahead, or to make more money—we then developed *those* gifts, meanwhile putting aside and forgetting the gifts which were neither so evident nor so valued by others. If our unused gifts have any strength or power of their own, they cry out for recognition—to be given a name. They are not only disturbers of our sleep; they make our days uneasy.[26]

Wherever we stand in life, God urges us to claim his gifts. In fact, he will probably trouble our spirits until we do. By his reckoning, no one is too young or too old to experience a blossoming of charismata. The only thing he demands of us is that we desire what he already gives. Even that, as Søren Kierkegaard saw quite clearly, may count as a charisma:

> The need [for the Holy Spirit] itself is a good and perfect gift from God, and the prayer about it is a good and perfect gift through God, and the communication of it is a good and perfect gift from above,

which comes down from the Father of lights, with whom is no variableness neither shadow of turning.[27]

The promise of God to his people (which means: to all who call upon him in need) is that his gifts abound. And so, therefore, may we.

NOTES

INTRODUCTION
Charismata: A Gracious Challenge?

1. John P. Kildahl, *The Psychology of Speaking in Tongues* (Harper & Row, Publishers, Inc., 1972), pp. 48–56.

2. Such a revolt against growing institutionalism in the church does seem to have characterized a second-century charismatic group called the Montanists, and this tendency no doubt plays some role in the contemporary movements. Nevertheless, the public policies of charismatic groups within the traditional denominations generally stress submission to pastors of local congregations and denominational officials, whether they show themselves sympathetic to charismatic practices or not.

3. All evidence points to a steady and continuing growth of the charismatic movements over the past twenty years. No peak is in sight. In 1973, for example, the now annual International Lutheran Conference on the Holy Spirit held in Minneapolis drew some 8,000 registered participants. By 1976 the number had swelled to over 25,000. See Erling T. Jorstad, *Bold in the Spirit: Lutheran Charismatic Renewal in America Today* (Augsburg Publishing House, 1974), p. 82; and W. Thorkelson, "The Year in Lutheranism," *Lutheran Brotherhood Bond,* Vol. 53 (Jan. 1977), p. 10. Last July, some 45,000 Protestants and Roman Catholics gathered in Kansas City for an ecumenical conference on charismatic renewal. See *Time,* Aug. 8, 1977, p. 43. *Time* editors estimate the number of charismatically oriented Christians now active in America's traditional churches to be about 5 million.

4. John Schütz correctly notes that in order for Biblical interpreters to grasp what is distinctive about Paul's understanding of the spiritual gifts, "it is necessary to get behind or beyond the charismatic personality to the charismatic property itself, inherently separable from the personality" (John H. Schütz, *Paul and the Anatomy of Apostolic Authority*, p. 274; Cambridge: At the University Press, 1975).

5. These words form part of the conclusion to Kierkegaard's first of three edifying discourses based on James 1:17. See *Edifying Discourses*, Vol. I, tr. by D. F. and L. M. Swenson (Augsburg Publishing House, 1943), pp. ix and 55.

6. *The Draft Proposed Book of Common Prayer* (The Seabury Press, Inc., 1977), pp. 364, 399. The phrase is an adaptation of a much earlier one, "the holy things *(ta hagia)* for the saints *(tois hagiois)*," which appears in Greek eucharistic liturgies at least as early as the fourth century. See Lucien Deiss (ed.), *Early Sources of the Liturgy* (Alba House, 1967), pp. 151, 179. My thanks go to Father Rhodes Cooper for pointing this out to me.

7. We should be aware that the New Testament writers never call the Eucharist itself a charisma. Paul, however, does reflect upon charismata in the context of words that may well have been used in early celebrations of the Lord's Supper. See Rom. 12:1-8, esp. v. 1.

8. Vinson Synan, *The Holiness-Pentecostal Movement in the United States* (Wm. B. Eerdmans Publishing Company, 1971), pp. 95–116.

9. Richard Quebedeaux, *The New Charismatics: The Origins, Development, and Significance of Neo-Pentecostalism* (Doubleday & Company, Inc., 1975), pp. 54ff.

10. *Ibid.*, pp. 63–68.

11. For a circumspect discussion of this issue and other historical-critical problems, see the appropriate sections in W. G. Kümmel, *Introduction to the New Testament*, revised and enlarged English edition, tr. by Howard Clark Kee (Abingdon Press, 1975).

12. *Ibid.,* pp. 156–185.

CHAPTER 1
Common and Special Gifts in the Old Testament

1. Another important reason for the popularity of certain psalms among early Christians was their use in interpreting Jesus' Christological identity. Psalms 2; 22; 69; and 110 especially were understood as having found their fulfillment in Jesus.

2. The reference is to Gerard Manley Hopkins' poem "God's Grandeur," found, among other places, in *The Oxford Book of Christian Verse,* ed. by Lord David Cecil (Oxford: At the Clarendon Press, 1951), p. 495.

3. Here, as in Num. 11:16ff. and 27:18ff., spirit is understood as a substance that can be transferred from one person to another. As in the Numbers passages, here too the initiative for the transfer and the means of accomplishing it reside in God alone (see II Kings 2:10–14). The Spirit-empowered individual never simply "decides" to pass on his or her gift to a successor.

4. Hannah's contention with God calls to mind the parable of the importunate widow in Luke 18:1–8. In both stories the lesson is that one "ought always to pray and not lose heart" (Luke 18:1).

5. Rom. 9:4 refers to these gifts as "the sonship, the glory, the covenants, the giving of the law, the worship, and the promises."

CHAPTER 2
Giftedness in the New Testament Church

1. The writer of the Fourth Gospel may be an exception to this rule. He does not seem to look forward to an imminent or even near return of Jesus to earth. When Jesus does "return," he will do so in order to take believers away from the world to the "Father's house" (John 14:1–3).

2. We are not certain that *these* passages were actually sung by individuals or groups in the early church, but Eph. 5:19f. indicates that the early church's worship did include the singing of "psalms and hymns and spiritual songs." On the other hand, what we have here called "hymns"

may have been spoken aloud as confessions, on the order of our Apostles' Creed. In any event, their rhythmic form strongly suggests a liturgical context.

3. Paul Schubert, *Form and Function of the Pauline Thanksgivings* (Berlin: Töpelmann, 1939), p. 184.

4. In order to examine this "explosion" of gift words in more detail, the reader may wish to consult an English concordance to the Bible such as *Young's Analytical Concordance* which lists New Testament passages containing words for "gift" and "give" in groups according to their Greek equivalents.

5. The practice of pronouncing verbal blessings upon people and material objects was a common one in first-century Judaism. Christians undoubtedly followed their Jewish brothers and sisters in speaking such *berakoth.*

CHAPTER 3
Holy Spirit: The Nearness of the Giver

1. Many scholars hold that Luke's account of Pentecost has become so overlaid with his own interpretation that we can no longer know just what happened. Idealized Luke's story certainly is; the speech he attributes to Peter reflects mostly his own theological concerns. Yet a corporate, even spectacular arrival of the Spirit much like the one he narrates must have occurred. Otherwise, we are at a loss to explain how shortly after the resurrection Jesus' bewildered, disorganized followers became a militant church, convinced that those who believed its preaching and underwent baptism would themselves manifest the gift of the Spirit. See the illuminating discussion of Pentecost in James D. G. Dunn, *Jesus and the Spirit* (The Westminster Press, 1975), pp. 136–152.

2. In II Tim. 1:6, a Pauline disciple, writing in the apostle's name, urges Timothy to "rekindle the gift (*charisma*) of God that is within you through the laying on of my hands." Here a reference to the Holy Spirit is probably intended (see v. 7).

3. Pentecostal and neo-Pentecostal Christians with whom I have spoken also resist the notion that they become ecstatically possessed while praying

in tongues. They feel that they retain a sense of will and a contact with the reality around them. Obviously, a nonrational experience need not be ecstatic in the sense that it wrenches one out of his or her normal psychosomatic state.

4. Arnold Come argues effectively for the view that what makes an individual truly human is his or her spirit. Come speaks of the human spirit as "the holy gift of 'the image of God.' " It is this which defines a particular mass of flesh and blood as a whole and inviolable person. See Arnold Come, *Human Spirit and Holy Spirit* (The Westminster Press, 1959), pp. 70–79, esp. p. 75.

5. Paul sometimes uses "flesh" as a neutral term denoting physical skin, muscles, etc. But in this context and in Rom., ch. 8, "flesh" is a pejorative term for everything adhering to our humanity that opposes God. For the psychic aspects of "flesh," see Gal. 5:19ff.

6. Arnold Bittlinger, *Gifts and Graces: A Commentary on 1 Corinthians 12–14* (Wm. B. Eerdmans Publishing Company, 1967), pp. 15–16.

7. Often we contemporary Christians properly find encouragement, via Biblical accounts of the Spirit, to articulate our own spiritual stories. Yet we should never impose upon ourselves the tyranny of expecting the two to be exactly the same. It is common and appropriate for believers to respond to Bible passages that grip them with something like, "Yes, my experience was *like* that, but at the same time more specific to my hopes and fears and therefore *unlike* the Biblical author's as well." Navy Chaplain William Olson judged his spiritual renewal to be authentic in large part because it met a long-felt need with such unexpected specificity: "Late one night in 1968, while [I was] reading a book about speaking in tongues by an Episcopalian scholar . . . , God revealed himself in a way I'd never experienced before. It came not so much as a distinct voice in my ear, but more like a sudden clearing of my mind. The verse seemed to flash before me, 'Then he opened their minds to understand the Scripture' (Luke 24:45). Now, I just knew this had to be from God, an unquestionable sign to me, for I'd never before in my life been able to recall Bible verses, and most especially not appropriate ones at crucial times. If God had *me* quoting the Bible, yes, something definitely was happening. It was telling me, 'Bill, now is the time; there is no other.' I said, 'OK,' as simple as that.

No lights flashed, no bells rang." (William G. Olson, *The Charismatic Church,* p. 25; Bethany Fellowship, Inc., 1974.)

8. See Chapter 5, pp. 128f.

9. Consider, e.g., the popularity of such recent books as Michael Korda, *Power: How to Get It, How to Use It* (Ballantine Books, Inc., 1976); and Robert Ringer, *Winning Through Intimidation* (Fawcett World Library, 1976).

10. Paul is our man here; intense first-person references to his own experience abound in his letters. If we want to know how it felt to be an early believer, we must give special attention to him rather than to Luke, most of whose reporting relies on tradition and is not very reflective by current standards.

11. Acts 13:52 seems to be the exception that proves the rule.

12. I Cor. 6:12–20 is probably directed against this syncretistic use of sexuality.

13. C. K. Barrett, *The First Epistle to the Corinthians* (Harper & Row, Publishers, Inc., 1968), pp. 279f.

14. See Frederick C. Grant, *Hellenistic Religions* (The Bobbs-Merrill Company, Inc., 1953), pp. 116–118.

15. Grant, *Hellenistic Religions,* pp. 121ff.

16. Franz Cumont, *Oriental Religions in Roman Paganism* (Dover Publications, 1956), pp. 105f.

17. E. Schweizer, "pneuma, pneumatikos," *Theological Dictionary of the New Testament,* ed. by Gerhard Kittel and Gerhard Friedrich, tr. by Geoffrey W. Bromiley (Wm. B. Eerdmans Publishing Company, 1971), Vol. VI, p. 345.

18. Eric R. Dodds, *The Greeks and the Irrational* (Beacon Press, Inc., 1957). The story was related to Plutarch by the prophet Nicander, a personal friend of his who was present at the event. Dodds claims that the

incident can be dated between A.D. 57 and 62, that is, during Paul's lifetime. See pp. 72f., 90n.59.

19. My translation is done from the Greek text edited by R. Flacelière (Paris: Société d'édition Les Belles Lettres, 1947).

20. In some cases, apparently, not even a memory of the possession was retained. See Dodds, *The Greeks and the Irrational*, p. 72.

21. Luke does record the leaping of John the Baptist in his mother's womb when the latter greets Mary with a Spirit-inspired blessing (Luke 1:41f.). He also notes in Acts that after the evangelist Philip had spoken to the Ethiopian eunuch, "the Spirit of the Lord caught up Philip; and the eunuch saw him no more" (Acts 8:39). But whatever these stories mean, they hardly reflect experiences typical among first-century believers.

22. It is not our intention to establish the Holy Spirit's uniqueness on the basis of historical evidence. Even if this were theoretically possible, we know too little about the ecstatic religions of the Hellenistic era to make such a claim. See, e.g., Dodds, *The Greeks and the Irrational*, p. 71.

CHAPTER 4

Renewal and Service Through Charismata

1. Since we are not presenting a lengthy description of the gifts in this context, the reader may wish to consult experiential treatments of them in such works by Pentecostal and neo-Pentecostal Christians as the following:

Bennett, Dennis J. *Nine O'Clock in the Morning* (Logos International, 1970).

Bittlinger, Arnold. *Gifts and Graces: A Commentary on 1 Corinthians 12–14* (Wm. B. Eerdmans Publishing Company, 1974).

Christenson, Larry. *Speaking in Tongues and Its Significance for the Church* (Bethany Fellowship, Inc., 1968).

Gee, Donald. *Spiritual Gifts in the Work of the Ministry Today* (Gospel Publishing House, 1963).

DuPlessis, David. *The Spirit Bade Me Go* (Logos International, 1970).

2. DuPlessis, *The Spirit Bade Me Go*, pp. 93–98.

3. See Schütz, *Paul and the Anatomy of Apostolic Authority*, p. 252.

4. DuPlessis, *The Spirit Bade Me Go*, p. 86.

5. The RSV translation of *charismata iamatōn* as "healers" (I Cor. 12:28) seems arbitrary, since the phrase literally means "gifts of healing," just as in vs. 9 and 30.

6. DuPlessis, *The Spirit Bade Me Go*, p. 95.

7. In his commentary on I Corinthians, Barrett notes that Paul's "point here seems . . . to be that some have the gift of celibacy and others, who lack this gift, and are therefore well advised to marry, have some other compensating gift or gifts." See Barrett, *The First Epistle to the Corinthians*, pp. 158f. But this "consolation prize" hypothesis is hardly convincing.

8. Philosophically, the term "supernatural" is quite problematic. We use it here simply to denote extraordinary phenomena that prove difficult to explain on the basis of what we know scientifically.

9. Gee, *Spiritual Gifts in the Work of the Ministry Today*, p. 10.

10. *Ibid.*, pp. 11–16.

11. *Ibid.*, p. 18. But we wonder whether this judgment applies also to speaking in tongues.

12. *Ibid.*, pp. 24, 29.

13. *Ibid.*, p. 19.

14. *Ibid.*, pp. 34f.

15. Bittlinger, *Gifts and Graces*, pp. 66, 70. See also Arnold Bittlinger, *Gifts and Ministries* (Wm. B. Eerdmans Publishing Company, 1973), p. 19.

16. Bittlinger, *Gifts and Graces*, p. 72.

17. *Ibid.*, p. 72.

18. E. E. Ellis " 'Spiritual' Gifts in the Pauline Community," *New Testament Studies,* Vol. 20 (1974), p. 129.

19. *Ibid.*, pp. 129f.

20. The term "individuation" occurs frequently in the psychology of C. G. Jung, where it refers to a "process in which the personality seeks to achieve wholeness." See Ann and Barry Ulanov, *Religion and the Unconscious* (The Westminster Press, 1975), p. 46. To my knowledge, Schütz is the first to use it to describe what Paul understands to be the effects of the charismata. See Schütz, *Paul and the Anatomy of Apostolic Authority,* p. 255.

21. John H. Schütz, "Charisma and Social Reality in Primitive Christianity," *Journal of Religion,* Vol. 54, No. 1 (1974), p. 60.

22. DuPlessis, *The Spirit Bade Me Go,* pp. 71f., 88f., 93–98. Merlin R. Carothers, *Prison to Praise: A Radical Prayer Concept for Changing Lives* (Charisma Books, 1971), p. 107.

23. Some neo-Pentecostal Christians find the latter term more acceptable. During a conference on the Holy Spirit held at Princeton Theological Seminary in 1974, Fr. Dennis Bennett cited John 7:38–39 as Biblical support for a dramatic upsurge of the Spirit in believers equivalent to what Luke calls baptism in the Spirit.

24. See I Cor. 12:13 and Frederick D. Bruner, *A Theology of the Holy Spirit: The Pentecostal Experience and the New Testament Witness* (Wm. B. Eerdmans Publishing Company, 1973), pp. 173–181.

25. Thus, when Paul discovers that a group of Ephesian disciples, having undergone only the baptism of John, do not yet know about the Holy Spirit, he has them baptized in the name of Jesus and, as a part of the baptismal rite, lays hands upon them. Immediately afterward, "the Holy Spirit came on them; and they spoke with tongues and prophesied" (Acts 19:6). See Bruner's helpful interpretation of Acts 19:1–7 on p. 211.

26. Ernst Käsemann, *An die Römer,* Handbuch zum Neuen Testament, 3d ed. (Tübingen: J. C. B. Mohr [Paul Siebeck], 1974), pp. 16f.

27. A similar "reappropriation" of gifts is mentioned in I Tim. 4:14, where the writer urges Timothy not to "neglect the gift *(charisma)* you have, which was given you by prophetic utterance when the council of elders laid their hands upon you," and in II Tim. 1:6f., where the author reminds his young reader to "rekindle the gift *(charisma)* of God that is within you through the laying on of my hands; for God did not give us a spirit of timidity but a spirit of power and love and self-control."

28. Krister Stendahl, "Glossolalia—The New Testament Evidence," in *Paul Among Jews and Gentiles* (Fortress Press, 1976), p. 120.

29. The Matthean parallel to this passage (Matt. 7:11) has "good things" in place of "Holy Spirit." Since Luke tends to highlight the work of the Spirit, we are probably dealing with his interpretation of Jesus' words. Perhaps he understood the disciples to be obeying this injunction by praying for the Spirit in the days immediately preceding Pentecost (Acts 1:14). Inasmuch as he was writing his Gospel to believers, however, he almost certainly intended the words of Jesus recorded in Luke 11:9–13 to have a wider application as well—namely, to all Christians.

30. C. K. Barrett, *The Second Epistle to the Corinthians* (Harper & Row, Publishers, Inc., 1973), pp. 57, 66–68.

31. Acts 8:17 and 19:6 refer to a laying on of hands in connection with the initial but delayed coming of the Spirit. In II Tim. 1:6 the Pauline author has in mind a physical contact that took place at the time of Timothy's baptism. By contrast, I Tim. 4:14 reminds Timothy of his "ordination," at which a charisma was transmitted "by prophetic utterance when the council of elders laid their hands upon you." This last passage does seem to refer to a charisma for ministry, received after the initial coming of the Spirit. But the laying on of hands was hardly understood by the earliest believers as normative for the reception of charismata in general. In I Cor., chs. 12 to 14, Paul says not a word to the congregation as a whole about receiving higher gifts through the hands of others. In fact, I Cor. 1:10–17 looks like a polemic against those who want to claim spiritual privileges on the basis of their water baptism by an illustrious Christian leader.

32. Paul even claims that God gives special honor to the weaker and inferior members of Christ's body, i.e., those who seem less gifted by human standards (I Cor. 12:24).

33. According to Mark 10:38f. and Luke 12:49f. Jesus anticipates a baptism which he and some of his disciples must undergo, but neither water nor the Spirit is mentioned. In both passages the context indicates that this baptism probably refers to suffering and death.

34. Throughout the Pauline corpus the Greek verb *baptizein* and the noun *baptisma* mean just one thing: water baptism (see Rom. 6:3, 4; I Cor. 1:13, 14, 15, 16, 17; 10:2; 15:29; Gal. 3:27; Eph. 4:5; Col. 2:12). Frederick D. Bruner's discussion of I Cor. 12:13 shows that it cannot be distinguished linguistically from other New Testament texts that speak of baptism *in* the Spirit (Matt. 3:11; Mark 1:8; Luke 3:16; John 1:33; Acts 1:5; 11:16). In other words, Paul thinks that water baptism and Spirit baptism usually occur simultaneously. See Bruner, *A Theology of the Holy Spirit,* pp. 291–295, esp. p. 293, n. 13. On the other hand, I Cor. 12:13 ("and all were made to drink of one Spirit") *may* refer to a manifestation of the Spirit prior to water baptism, namely, to the Corinthians' conversion (I Cor. 2:1–5; 12:3). But this is not viewed by Paul as a baptism.

35. That believers often feel a new sense of fullness in the Spirit when receiving a charisma is certainly not disputed. Paul speaks frequently of the joy, peace, and power brought by the Spirit even apart from his talk about charismata. See, e.g., Rom. 14:17; 15:13. On the other hand, as we shall discover in Chapter 5, the reception and practice of charismata do not always produce such buoyancy.

36. We refer to Paul's celibacy (I Cor. 7:7). Was this a gift disclosed to Paul alone, or not? We have too little information for a firm answer. Experientially, it is the case that some individuals affiliated with contemporary movements for spiritual renewal have received the charisma of tongues in moments of privacy. But this usually happens after they have spent some time with a group that practices tongues.

37. Elizabeth O'Connor, *Eighth Day of Creation* (Word Books, 1975), pp. 8–9.

38. *Ibid.,* p. 52.

39. *The Oxford Book of Christian Verse,* pp. 147f.

CHAPTER 5
The Gift of the Cross

1. John Sherrill, *They Speak with Other Tongues* (Fleming H. Revell Company, 1965), pp. 124ff.

2. *Ibid.,* p. 126.

3. *Ibid.,* pp. 127, 132.

4. See Ernst Käsemann, "The Cry for Liberty in the Worship of the Church" in *Perspectives on Paul,* tr. by Margaret Kohl (Fortress Press, 1971), pp. 127–137.

5. *Ibid.,* pp. 135f.

6. My personal talks with neo-Pentecostals have confirmed this Pauline interpretation. They have told me that two kinds of situations call forth their prayer in tongues with greatest frequency: times of plenty, for which they wish to thank God, and periods of intense need, during which they feel moved to confess their own hollowness.

7. The incorporation of weakness into a believer's charismatic life became a major issue in II Corinthians where Paul, an "earthen vessel" (II Cor. 4:7), found himself competing against "superapostles" (II Cor. 11:5, 12–15; 12:11f.), whose gospel offered the Corinthians a painless and ever-increasing spiritual power. See especially II Cor., chs. 10 to 13.

8. The most convincing discussion of this thorn I know occurs in E. Güttgemanns, *Der leidende Apostel und sein Herr* (Göttingen: Vandenhoeck und Ruprecht, 1966), pp. 162–165.

9. Henri Nouwen, *The Wounded Healer* (Doubleday & Company, Inc., 1972), p. 89.

10. Käsemann, *An die Römer,* p. 224.

11. For myself, it has become necessary to understand radical, undeserved suffering as a combination of human responsibility and demonic powers. Personal healing is always possible; so is societal reformation. Moral vigilance may defend certain levels of existence from the powers for a time. But despite our "progress," they eventually creep back in, especially through our pride. In my view, the novels of Charles Williams, e.g., *Descent Into Hell,* and Walker Percy's Kierkegaardian masterpiece *Love in the Ruins,* along with such imaginative works by C. S. Lewis as *The Screwtape Letters* and *That Hideous Strength,* witness effectively to the presence of satanic activity in today's world. I also find quite plausible the theological-political analysis of American culture in William Stringfellow's *An Ethic for Christians and Other Aliens in a Strange Land.* Like the other authors cited above, he makes frequent reference to the demonic.

12. C. S. Lewis, *Surprised by Joy: The Shape of My Early Life* (Harcourt, Brace and Company, Inc., 1955), p. 238.

13. Some scholars maintain that our Philippians is a composite of three shorter Pauline letters. See Kümmel, *Introduction to the New Testament,* pp. 332ff. For our purposes, the truth of the composite theory matters little, since the same relationship between joy and suffering prevails in all three of the alleged fragments.

CHAPTER 6
From Gift to Task to Giver

1. To a large extent our discussion grows out of Ernst Käsemann's work on this topic. See especially "Ministry and Community in the New Testament" and "The Pauline Doctrine of the Lord's Supper" in *Essays on New Testament Themes,* tr. by W. J. Montague (London: SCM Press, 1964), pp. 63–94, 113–119; and "Worship in Everyday Life: A Note on Romans 12" in *New Testament Questions of Today,* tr. by W. J. Montague (Fortress Press, 1969), pp. 188–195.

2. Our drawing breaks down if it is understood as a graph of God's relative distance from us. He is always near. The diagram attempts to picture our consciousness of him.

3. Paul is also quite conscious of love's necessity as he writes Rom. 12: 1ff. See vs. 9ff.

4. Edward G. Selwyn, *The First Epistle of St. Peter* (London: Macmillan and Co., Ltd., 1961), p. 217.

5. The same idea of love's motion from God, through us to others, and back again to God occurs throughout I John.

6. O'Connor, *Eighth Day of Creation,* p. 10.

7. *Ibid.,* pp. 24, 32–34.

8. John V. Taylor, *The Go-Between God* (Fortress Press, 1973).

9. William Stringfellow, *An Ethic for Christians and Other Aliens in a Strange Land.* (Word Books, 1973). See especially pp. 117–157.

10. *Ibid.,* pp. 138–140.

11. Elizabeth O'Connor is also quite clear about this. She writes: "We cannot exercise our gifts and at the same time be defenders of the status quo. Our gifts put us in tension with things as they are" (*Eighth Day of Creation,* p. 49). See, in addition, Paul S. Minear's helpful chapter on "The Prophetic Vocation Today" in his book *To Heal and to Reveal: The Prophetic Vocation According to Luke* (The Seabury Press, Inc., 1976), pp. 148–166.

12. Any social ethic based on the New Testament must face the fact that the canonical authors see charismata as aids for bringing the world into the church. Above all, the first believers wished to introduce or reintroduce people to their God. Of course this in itself was a revolutionary program fraught with political overtones. See Acts 17:6–7.

13. Käsemann, *Essays on New Testament Themes,* pp. 116–119.

14. The same Greek stem *anakain-* is used for "renewal" in both passages, the only places it appears in Paul's genuine writings. Moreover, in Rom. 7:22–25 "mind" and "inner man" are clearly interchangeable.

15. Käsemann, following Paul, emphasizes the Lord's gracious judgment of the believer in the Supper. See *Essays on New Testament Themes,* pp. 124–127.

16. Here, as in I Cor. 12:1 and 14:1, *pneumatika* probably means "spiritual *gifts.*" Even though the undefined neuter plural could mean "spiritual truths" (I Cor. 9:11), the context of our passage shows that Paul has in mind things *given (ta charisthenta,* v. 12). In a sense, the entire letter could be entitled "Interpreting Spiritual Gifts"; I Cor. 1:4–9 would be the prologue that sets Paul's agenda. *Ta charisthenta* probably refers, in part, to the future gifts of I Cor. 2:9, but again the context indicates that its primary meaning is gifts presently enjoyed (see vs. 13–16).

17. Walter Bauer, *A Greek-English Lexicon of the New Testament and Other Early Christian Literature,* tr. and adapted by William F. Arndt and F. Wilbur Gingrich (The University of Chicago Press, 1957), p. 559.

18. Erwin Prange, *The Gift Is Already Yours* (Logos International, 1973). See especially pp. 51–53.

19. But neither is it a condemnation or an attempt to dissuade those already affiliated. I owe many debts of gratitude to neo-Pentecostal friends. It is one thing to question a group's interpretation of its experience and quite another to declare the experience itself illegitimate, sick, or demonic. We are not making the second judgment.

20. Paul Minear, for example, sees the public Sunday morning confession of sins by a congregation as potentially charismatic. (*To Heal and to Reveal,* p. 160.)

21. The rich phrase in quotation marks comes from Henri Nouwen. See *The Wounded Healer, passim.*

CHAPTER 7

Charismata and Charismatics

1. Paul's sarcastic blast against the Corinthians in I Cor. 4:8 ("Already you are filled *(kekoresmenoi)*! Already you have become rich! Without us you have become kings! And would that you did reign, so that we might

share the rule with you!") intends to attack not their *experience* of charismatic fullness—for this he thanks God quite unreservedly in I Cor. 1:4–7 —but their interpretation and practice of it (see chs. 5ff. in I Corinthians). Bruner's otherwise careful exegetical critique of Pentecostal theology suffers from a lack of attention to the common experiential ground that Paul holds with the Corinthians. Bruner seems to think that Paul commends his theology of the cross as a substitute for charismatic fullness. See *A Theology of the Holy Spirit,* pp. 303–319. Actually, the apostle considers it a necessary part of that fullness. He does not stress the *hiddenness* of spiritual power nearly so much as its *manifestation* through one's participation in the weakness, suffering, and death of Christ (I Cor. 2:1–5; 4:9–21; II Cor. 4:7–12; 12:9–10; 13:1–4; Phil. 3:10). Nor does Paul talk "only reluctantly of [charismatic] signs" as a validation of his ministry (Bruner, *A Theology of the Holy Spirit,* p. 315). See, e.g., I Cor. 2:4f.; 14:18; II Cor. 3:3; 5:13; 12:12f.; Rom. 15:18–19; Gal. 3:1–5.

2. Paul Minear sees in Luke-Acts "an account of the training of apprentice seers and exorcists." (*To Heal and to Reveal,* pp. 148f.)

3. Sherrill, *They Speak with Other Tongues,* pp. 127f.

4. *Ibid.* and Larry Christenson, "Two Keys to Lordship: Discipleship and Headship," *Lutheran Charismatic Renewal Newsletter,* Vol. 1, No. 6 (May 1975), p. 3.

5. I hasten to add that most of my personal relationships with Pentecostals and neo-Pentecostals have been quite free of these hidden demands.

6. Larry Christenson, *The Christian Family* (Bethany Fellowship, Inc., 1970), pp. 17–18, 32.

7. *Ibid.,* pp. 32–54.

8. Of the four women most often cited by Richard Quebedeaux as prominent in the movement (Josephine M. Ford, the late Kathryn Kuhlman, Catherine Marshall, and Jean Stone) not one could be considered a pastoral leader within a congregation. Professor Ford, who teaches New Testament at the University of Notre Dame, broke with the Roman Catholic charismatic community there a few years ago, in part over the issue

of male dominance. Melodyland Christian Center in Anaheim, California, a leading church and graduate training center in the Protestant neo-Pentecostal movement, "neither ordains women nor permits them membership on its governing board." See *The New Charismatics,* p. 110 and notes 16–17. On the issue of women's status in the church classical Pentecostal believers have shown themselves generally more flexible than their younger cousins. The Assemblies of God, one of the largest Pentecostal denominations in the U.S.A., has recognized a pastoral ministry for women since 1918, four years after its inception. By 1920 roughly a third of its ordained ministers were female! According to Vinson Synan, "the pentecostals by the middle of the twentieth century probably had more women preachers than any other branch of Christianity." See *The Holiness-Pentecostal Movement in the United States,* p. 188. On the other hand, a major Pentecostal denomination, the largely black Church of God in Christ, does not presently ordain women.

9. Robin Scroggs, "Paul and the Eschatological Woman," *Journal of the American Academy of Religion,* Vol. XL, No. 3 (Sept. 1972), pp. 294ff.

10. Krister Stendahl *The Bible and the Role of Women,* tr. by Emilie T. Sander (Fortress Press, 1966), pp. 32ff.

11. Scroggs argues that I Cor. 14:33–36, which appears to countermand I Cor. 11:2–16 and can easily be removed without disturbing the context, ought to be considered an interpolation into the letter by a late-first-century editor for the purpose of harmonizing I Corinthians with I Tim. 2:12ff. See "Paul and the Eschatological Woman," p. 284. On the other hand, if Paul is the author, he probably intended to put a damper on what he feared might become an unnecessary offense to both Jewish and Gentile observers of the church, namely, the "disruption" of public worship by the noisy questioning of wives, whom society at large considered subordinate to their husbands.

12. In my view, we ought to give Paul's tension-filled thinking clear preference over the regressive, old creation resolutions of his disciples in I Timothy and Titus. He at least wrestled with the fact that the turn of the ages had begun to affect the fundamental structures of society (see I Cor. 7:25–35).

13. Luke seems to have added the phrase "the last days," for it does not occur in Joel 2:28–32. Luke probably conceived of these last days as an extended period of time—decades at least—during the course of which the gospel would penetrate all corners of the world.

14. J. Rodman Williams, *The Era of the Spirit: Barth, Brunner, Tillich and Bultmann on the Holy Spirit* (Logos International, 1971), pp. 58–59. Compare Williams' slightly less enthusiastic statements in his later book, *The Pentecostal Reality* (Logos International, 1972), pp. 29, 52–54.

15. James W. Jones, *The Spirit and the World* (Hawthorn Books, Inc., 1975), pp. 71–72.

16. *Ibid.*, p. 76.

17. *Ibid.*, p. 77.

18. Jorstad, *Bold in the Spirit: Lutheran Charismatic Renewal in America Today,* p. 84.

19. *Ibid.*, p. 85.

20. David Wilkerson, *Racing Toward Judgment* (Fleming H. Revell Company, 1976), p. 8.

21. I count only two references to Revelation (Rev. 3:17 on p. 21 and Rev. 18:7 on p. 90), neither of them characteristic of the book's pervasive interest in futuristic prophecy.

22. Wilkerson, *Racing Toward Judgment,* p. 70.

23. *Ibid.*, pp. 115–116.

24. See *ibid.*, pp. 67, 70f., 76f., 81.

25. Barrett, *The First Epistle to the Corinthians,* p. 380.

26. O'Connor, *Eighth Day of Creation,* p. 31.

27. These words conclude the second of Søren Kierkegaard's three edifying discourses written on James 1:17–21. See *Edifying Discourses,* Vol. II, tr. by D. F. and L. M. Swenson (Augsburg Publishing House, 1950), p. 44.

INDEX